Welcome to Your
Texas State Parks Adventure!

Welcome to your ultimate guide to the natural wonders of the Lone Star State! Whether you're a seasoned explorer or just beginning to discover the beauty of Texas, this book is your companion for visiting every official State Park and Historic Site.

Inside, you'll find everything you need to plan your adventures—from historical background and park highlights to trail details and fun facts. Organized by region, this guide is designed to help you make the most of every visit, whether you're chasing waterfalls in Central Texas or birdwatching along the Gulf Coast.

So grab your hiking boots, pack your picnic, and let this book guide you to unforgettable moments across Texas. Each park visit is a story waiting to be written.

Join the Community!
Want to connect with other park lovers?

Join us on Instagram
@wanderstamped

Tag us & share photos, tips, stamp progress, and trip recommendations with fellow adventurers across the state. We'd love to see where your journey takes you!

See you on the trails, and happy exploring!

–The Wander Stamped Family

Before You Wander

This book is designed to help you explore Texas State Parks with ease, inspiration, and confidence. Each park page includes historical background, highlighted trails, fun facts, and spaces to document your experience.

You'll find a spot for the official park stamp and a photo space sized to fit a 2x3 print from your visit. Wallet sized prints work perfectly for this visual memory journal.

While we highlight top trails for each park, not all trails are listed due to space limitations. Each page includes a QR code that links directly to the Texas Parks & Wildlife website, giving you up-to-date information on trail systems, park alerts, and maps.

Because park conditions and policies can change, it's essential to check updates before each visit. Hours, entrance fees, closures, and facility availability may vary throughout the year. We strongly encourage you to scan the QR codes or visit the official site to check for alerts, such as fire bans or weather-related closures.

At the time of publication, the following parks were not yet open to the public:

- Albert & Bessie Kronkosky State Natural Area
- Powderhorn State Park
- Bear Creek State Park

Pages for these parks are included so you can add information as it becomes available.

We hope this book becomes your go-to guide for making lifelong memories in nature. Here's to your Texas adventure—one park at a time.

Texas State Parks by Region

Table of Contents & Stamp Checklist

(Check each box as you visit and stamp your way across the state!)

Texas State Parks by Region

Table of Contents & Stamp Checklist

(Check each box as you visit and stamp your way across the state!)

Bonham State Park

1363 State Park 24, Bonham, TX 75418   -   Hours: Open daily from 8 AM to 10 PM

2X3 photo

History

Bonham State Park **opened in 1936** and is a legacy of the Civilian Conservation Corps (CCC), which developed the park between 1933 and 1936. CCC Company 894 constructed the dam, created the 65-acre lake, and built the park's signature rustic structures — many of which are still in use. The area was historically used for farming, and the CCC planted thousands of trees to restore the land and create a natural retreat for nearby communities.

The park's design follows the naturalistic planning style of the era, blending stonework, trails, and scenic overlooks seamlessly into the North Texas landscape.

Top Trails & Sites Visited

- ☐ Lake Loop Trail (1.3 mi)
- ☐ Armadillo Hill Trail (1.5 mi)
- ☐ Bois d'Arc Trail (2.7 mi)
- ☐ Gnarly Root Trail (1.3 mi)
- ☐ CCC Footbridge
- ☐ Other: _______________________

Date of Visit: ____

Where did you stay? ____

Who were you with? ____

What did you do? ____

Favorite Memories? ____

____

____

State Park Stamp

Interesting Facts

- The park's 65-acre lake was hand-dug and filled by the CCC using early dam construction methods.
- You can rent single or tandem kayaks on weekends during the warmer seasons.
- Home to one of Texas' oldest CCC-built picnic pavilions, still available for use today.
- The park has two group barracks facilities, ideal for scouts, reunions, or school trips.
- Wildlife sightings often include armadillos, red foxes, and barred owls.

Park Website   Park Maps

Visit the Texas Parks & Wildlife Department at tpwd.texas.gov

Cedar Hill State Park

1570 FM 1382, Cedar Hill, TX 75104 - Hours: Open daily from 6 AM to 10 PM

2X3 photo

History

Cedar Hill State Park **opened in 1991** and offers a slice of Hill Country landscape just 20 minutes from downtown Dallas. The park sits along the eastern edge of Joe Pool Lake, a reservoir completed in the 1980s for water supply, flood control, and recreation.

The area preserves limestone hills, native prairie, and forested trails, providing a natural escape in a rapidly urbanizing part of Texas. One of its unique features is the Penn Farm Agricultural History Center, which preserves restored buildings and artifacts from a family farm dating back to the mid-1800s.

Top Trails & Sites Visited

☐ Duck Pond Trail (0.8 mi)
☐ Shoreline Trail (1.0 mi)
☐ Talala Trail (2.3 mi)
☐ DORBA Trail System (3–12 mi)
☐ Penn Farm Trail (0.6 mi)
☐ Other: _______________________

Date of Visit: ____

Where did you stay? ____

Who were you with? ____

What did you do? ____

Favorite Memories? ____

____

____

Interesting Facts

- The Penn Farm Agricultural Center offers a walking tour through barns, a windmill, and early farming equipment.
- Cedar Hill lies within the White Rock Escarpment, a geological fault zone with exposed limestone.
- The park is a birding hotspot, especially during spring and fall migrations.
- Joe Pool Lake is ideal for boating, jet skiing, swimming, and fishing.

State Park Stamp

Park Website

Park Maps

Cleburne State Park

5800 Park Road 21, Cleburne, TX 76033   -   Hours: Open daily from 6 AM to 10 PM

2X3 photo

History

Cleburne State Park was built by the Civilian Conservation Corps (CCC) in the 1930s and **opened in 1939**. The CCC constructed the park's signature 116-acre spring-fed Cedar Lake by building an earthen dam on Camp Creek. The land had previously been used for ranching and small-scale farming. Many of the original CCC-built stone structures and roads remain in use today, showcasing their craftsmanship.

The park's limestone hills, hardwood forests, and scenic lake have made it a long-time favorite for hikers, mountain bikers, and families looking for a wooded escape near the DFW metroplex.

Top Trails & Sites Visited

- ☐ Spillway Trail (0.7 mi)
- ☐ Coyote Run Nature Trail (1.1 mi)
- ☐ Camp Creek Loop (1.1 mi)
- ☐ White-Tail Hollow Trail (1.7 mi)
- ☐ Park Road 21 Overlook
- ☐ Other: _______________________

Date of Visit: ____

Where did you stay? ____

Who were you with? ____

What did you do? ____

Favorite Memories? ____

____

____

State Park Stamp

Interesting Facts

- Cedar Lake is spring-fed, giving it clearer water than many other North Texas lakes.
- The park has 13+ miles of multi-use trails, popular with mountain bikers.
- White-tailed deer, armadillos, and barred owls are often spotted near campsites.
- The CCC-built spillway and bridge are still in use and photograph-worthy.
- In spring, the park bursts with bluebonnets, Indian paintbrushes, and other native wildflowers.

Park Website

Park Maps

Visit the Texas Parks & Wildlife Department at tpwd.texas.gov

Cooper Lake State Park

South Sulphur: 1690 FM 3505, Sulphur Springs, TX 75482
Doctors Creek: 1664 FM 1529 South, Cooper, TX 75432

Hours: Open daily from 6 AM to 10 PM

2X3 photo

History

Cooper Lake State Park was **established in the mid-1990s** following the construction of Jim Chapman Lake, commonly known as Cooper Lake, a U.S. Army Corps of Engineers reservoir completed in 1991. The park preserves more than 3,000 acres split between two distinct units: Doctors Creek (north side) and South Sulphur (south side).

This region of Texas was historically inhabited by Caddo peoples and later became cattle and cotton country. Today, the lake and surrounding oak woodlands offer an escape into nature for campers, anglers, equestrians, and paddlers.

Top Trails & Sites Visited

- ☐ Cedar Creek North Loop (0.6 mi)
- ☐ Cedar Creek South Loop (0.5 mi)
- ☐ Coyote Run Trail (4.6 mi)
- ☐ Terrace Trail (0.3 mi)
- ☐ Other: ___________________________
- ☐ Other: ___________________________

Date of Visit: _______________________________________

Where did you stay? _______________________________________

Who were you with? _______________________________________

What did you do? _______________________________________

Favorite Memories? _______________________________________

____

Interesting Facts

- The park is split into two full-service units — both with camping, swimming, and fishing access.
- You can ride horses on over 10 miles of equestrian trails at the South Sulphur Unit.
- Doctors Creek Unit is known for its peaceful RV campsites and lakeside breezes.
- South Sulphur offers furnished cabins and screened shelters for non-tent campers.
- The lake is stocked with catfish, crappie, bass, and hybrid striped bass.

State Park Stamp

Park Website

Park Maps

Visit the Texas Parks & Wildlife Department at tpwd.texas.gov

Dinosaur Valley State Park

1629 Park Road 59, Glen Rose, TX 76043   -   Hours: Open daily from 7 AM to 10 PM

2X3 photo

History

Dinosaur Valley State Park was **established in 1972** to preserve prehistoric dinosaur tracks found in the bed of the Paluxy River. These fossilized footprints, made by theropods and sauropods, were first documented in the early 1900s. The land was once part of a ranching operation before being acquired by the state.

In addition to its fossil history, the park features rolling limestone hills, hardwood forests, and scenic views of the Paluxy River Valley. Two large dinosaur sculptures near the park entrance were originally built for the 1964 New York World's Fair and later relocated here.

Top Trails & Sites Visited

- ☐ Main Track Site Trail (0.5 mi)
- ☐ Overlook Trail (1.3 mi)
- ☐ Paluxy River Trail (2.0 mi)
- ☐ Dinosaur Models & Tracks
- ☐ Oak Springs Trail (0.3 mi)
- ☐ Other: _______________________

Date of Visit: ____

Where did you stay? ____

Who were you with? ____

What did you do? ____

Favorite Memories? ____

____

____

State Park Stamp

Interesting Facts

- The park has five main dinosaur track sites, visible when river levels are low.
- A mobile app and QR codes help visitors find and identify track locations.
- You can wade or walk in the actual riverbed where dinosaurs stepped millions of years ago.
- Horseback riding trails are available (bring your own horse).
- The park hosts stargazing and fossil-themed ranger events throughout the year.

Park Website

Park Maps

Visit the Texas Parks & Wildlife Department at tpwd.texas.gov

Eisenhower State Park

50 Park Road 20, Denison, TX 75020 - Hours: Open daily from 8 AM to 10 PM

2X3 photo

History

Eisenhower State Park was **established in 1958** and named after President Dwight D. Eisenhower, who was born in nearby Denison, Texas. The park is located on the southern shore of Lake Texoma, one of the largest reservoirs in the U.S., built in 1944 by damming the Red River. The area was originally inhabited by various Indigenous groups and later became a hotspot for frontier settlements.

Today, the park is known for its rugged limestone cliffs, scenic lake views, and popular fishing coves. The terrain includes hardwood forest, open prairie, and shoreline bluffs — offering a unique slice of North Texas nature.

Top Trails & Sites Visited

- ☐ Armadillo Hill Trail (0.8 mi)
- ☐ Ammonite Crossing
- ☐ Ike's Hike and Bike Trail (3.2 mi)
- ☐ Overlook Trail (3.6 mi)
- ☐ Lover's Leap
- ☐ Other: _______________________

Date of Visit: _______________________

Where did you stay? _______________________

Who were you with? _______________________

What did you do? _______________________

Favorite Memories? _______________________

Interesting Facts

- Home to scenic limestone bluffs overlooking Lake Texoma.
- Features designated ATV and off-road bike trails, rare among Texas parks.
- The Ammonite Crossing highlights fossils and marine history from an ancient sea.
- Offers lighted fishing piers, a marina, and swimming areas.
- Hosts an annual kids' fish day and frequent ranger programs.

State Park Stamp

Park Website

Park Maps

Fort Richardson State Park & Historic Site

228 State Park Rd 61, Jacksboro, TX 76458   -   Hours: Open daily from 8 AM to 5 PM

2X3 photo

History

Established in 1968, Fort Richardson State Park preserves the remnants of a U.S. Army fort built in 1867 to protect settlers from raids during westward expansion. It was once the largest U.S. military installation in Texas, home to Buffalo Soldiers, infantry units, and frontier scouts.

The fort played a key role in the Indian Wars, serving as a base for campaigns across the West. Abandoned by the military in 1878, many original buildings remained, including a hospital, guardhouse, magazine, bakery, and officers' quarters — several of which are now fully restored and open for guided tours.

Top Trails & Sites Visited

- ☐ Lost Creek Reservoir State Trailway (9 mi)
- ☐ Oak Ridge Trail (0.4 mi)
- ☐ Kicking Bird Trail (0.3 mi)
- ☐ Rumbling Spring
- ☐ Flour Mill View
- ☐ Other: _______________________

Date of Visit: ____

Where did you stay? ____

Who were you with? ____

What did you do? ____

Favorite Memories? ____

____

____

State Park Stamp

Interesting Facts

- The guardhouse at Fort Richardson was known for its extreme disciplinary measures — and still stands today.
- Visitors can tour seven original and restored fort buildings, with exhibits and furnishings.
- The park includes a section of the Lost Creek Reservoir State Trailway, ideal for hikers and cyclists.
- It's a great site for living history events, featuring reenactors in 1800s uniforms.
- Fort Richardson was designated a National Historic Landmark in 1963.

Park Website   Park Maps

Visit the Texas Parks & Wildlife Department at tpwd.texas.gov

Lake Mineral Wells State Park

100 Park Road 71, Mineral Wells, TX 76067   -   Hours: Open daily from 6 AM to 10 PM

2X3 photo

History

Lake Mineral Wells State Park **opened in 1981** to protect the historic water supply reservoir that served the town of Mineral Wells starting in 1922. The area is known for its connection to the Texas & Pacific Railroad, whose rail line was later converted into the 20-mile Lake Mineral Wells Trailway — part of the Rails-to-Trails Conservancy initiative.

The park is famous for its rock climbing area at Penitentiary Hollow, one of the few natural climbing spots in North Texas. The surrounding forest and lake make it a popular escape for hikers, equestrians, and outdoor adventurers.

Top Trails & Sites Visited

☐ Cross Timbers Black Trail (2.3 mi)
☐ Red Waterfront Trail (0.8 mi)
☐ Trailway Spur (0.6 mi)
☐ Blue Waterfront Trail (1.5 mi)
☐ Penitentiary Hollow Overlook
☐ Other: _______________________

Date of Visit: ____

Where did you stay? ____

Who were you with? ____

What did you do? ____

Favorite Memories? ____

____

____

Interesting Facts

- Penitentiary Hollow is a unique natural sandstone climbing canyon.
- The Trailway extends 20 miles and is open to hikers, bikers, and horseback riders.
- Home to historical remnants of the Weatherford, Mineral Wells & Northwestern Railway.
- The lake is stocked for catfish, sunfish, and largemouth bass.

State Park Stamp

Park Website   Park Maps

Visit the Texas Parks & Wildlife Department at tpwd.texas.gov

Palo Pinto Mountains State Park

1915 State Highway 16 South, Strawn, TX 76475 - Hours: Open daily from 8 AM to 10 PM

2X3 photo

History

Palo Pinto Mountains State Park is the first new large-scale Texas state park to open in over 25 years. Acquired by the state in 2011 and **officially opened in 2026**, the park spans over 4,800 acres of scenic hills, grasslands, and lakes west of Fort Worth.

The area was once ranchland and contains rolling hills, spring-fed creeks, and Lake Tucker, a 90-acre reservoir at the heart of the park. TPWD developed the site with minimal infrastructure to preserve the wild, natural character of the region while offering modern-day hiking, biking, paddling, and equestrian access.

Top Trails & Sites Visited

☐
☐
☐
☐
☐ Other: _______________________
☐ Other: _______________________

Date of Visit: ____

Where did you stay? ____

Who were you with? ____

What did you do? ____

Favorite Memories? ____

____

____

State Park Stamp

Interesting Facts

- Lake Tucker is open for kayaking, canoeing, and fishing — no motorboats allowed.
- The park features 15+ miles of brand-new trails, open to hikers, bikers, and horseback riders.
- Its location makes it a dark sky haven for stargazing west of DFW.
- Wildlife sightings include turkey, white-tailed deer, armadillos, and bobcats.
- It was one of the most requested new parks during Texas' 100-Year State Parks celebration.

Park Website

Park Maps

Visit the Texas Parks & Wildlife Department at tpwd.texas.gov

Possum Kingdom State Park

3901 State Park Rd. 33, Caddo, TX 76429   – Hours: Open daily from 6 AM to 10 PM

2X3 photo

History

Possum Kingdom State Park **opened in 1950** on the shores of Possum Kingdom Lake, a massive reservoir created by the construction of Morris Sheppard Dam in the 1940s. The parkland was developed with help from the Civilian Conservation Corps (CCC), who built early roads, trails, and infrastructure.

The lake, spanning over 17,000 acres, is known for its deep, clear blue waters, rugged limestone cliffs, and popular coves. The park continues to be one of the most visited spots in North Central Texas for boating, fishing, and camping.

Top Trails & Sites Visited

☐ Lakeview Trail (1.4 mi)
☐ Longhorn Trail (0.4 mi)
☐ Chaparral Ridge Trail (0.5 mi)
☐ Fish Sculpture
☐ Other: _______________________
☐ Other: _______________________

Date of Visit: ____

Where did you stay? ____

Who were you with? ____

What did you do? ____

Favorite Memories? ____

____

____

Interesting Facts

- The lake is home to the famous "Hell's Gate" cliffs, a popular gathering and photo spot (though just outside park boundaries).
- Possum Kingdom has some of the clearest water of any Texas reservoir.
- The lake's name came from a 19th-century fur trader who called the area his "possum kingdom" due to the abundance of pelts.
- The park offers air-conditioned cabins just steps from the lake.

State Park Stamp

Park Website

Park Maps

Purtis Creek State Park

14225 FM 316 N, Eustace, TX 75124   –   Hours: Open daily from 6 AM to 10 PM

2X3 photo

History

Opened in 1988, Purtis Creek was established to preserve and showcase the 1,582-acre reservoir created in 1980 for flood control. The land was purchased from private owners in 1977.

The park includes remnants of Native American (Wichita & Caddo) settlement and 19th-century farmland. It was envisioned as a multi-use destination with areas for fishing, boating, and camping using sustainable design principles. Today, it balances outdoor recreation with conservation of oak-hickory upland, freshwater lake habitat, and woodland trails.

Top Trails & Sites Visited

- ☐ Solar Walk Trail (0.5 mi)
- ☐ Harmony Hill Picnic Area
- ☐ Beaver Slide Nature Path (1.3 mi)
- ☐ Wolfpen Hike & Bike Trail (0.8 mi)
- ☐ Bent by Nature Tree
- ☐ Other: _______________________

Date of Visit: ____

Where did you stay? _______________________________________

Who were you with? _______________________________________

What did you do? ____

Favorite Memories? _______________________________________

____

State Park Stamp

Interesting Facts

- The park lends out rods, reels, and tackle boxes, making it easy for families to fish without bringing gear.
- Beaver Slide Nature Path (1.7 mi) hugs the lakeshore for scenic walks.
- Solar Trail is a short, paved, wheelchair-accessible path along the dam.
- Kayaks/canoes are rentable from a self-serve kiosk, no staff needed.
- The park provides a free all-terrain wheelchair to visitors upon request.

Park Website

Park Maps

Visit the Texas Parks & Wildlife Department at tpwd.texas.gov

Ray Roberts Lake State Park

2X3 photo

History

Ray Roberts Lake State Park was created following the construction of Ray Roberts Lake, a reservoir formed in the 1980s by damming the Elm Fork of the Trinity River. The park officially **opened in 1993** to preserve recreation and natural areas around the lake's 29,000-acre shoreline. It's named after Ray Roberts, a Texas legislator who played a key role in water resource legislation.

The park is split into **three distinct sections**:

- Isle du Bois (east side of the lake),
- Johnson Branch (west side), and
- the Greenbelt Corridor, a linear trail and waterway stretching south toward Lake Lewisville.

These units offer a mix of forested trails, equestrian routes, beaches, and camping.

Top Trails & Sites Visited

- ☐ Eagle Activity Trail (0.3 mi)
- ☐ Lost Pines Trail (0.5 mi)
- ☐ Randy Bell Scenic Trail (2.2 mi)
- ☐ Other: _______________________

Date of Visit: ____

Where did you stay? ____

Who were you with? ____

What did you do? ____

Favorite Memories? ____

____

Interesting Facts

- The Greenbelt Corridor includes over 20 miles of trails for hiking, biking, and horseback riding.
- Isle du Bois features one of the most popular swimming beaches in the North Texas state park system.
- The lake is stocked with largemouth bass, catfish, and crappie — and hosts fishing tournaments.
- The park is home to the Denton County Wildlife Management Area, protecting critical habitat.
- Equestrian-friendly trails and trailer parking are available in both the Greenbelt and Johnson Branch units.

State Park Stamp

Park Website   Park Maps

Atlanta State Park

927 Park Road 42, Atlanta, TX 75551   -   Hours: Open daily from 6 AM to 10 PM

2X3 photo

History

Established in 1954 on land leased from the Department of the Army, Atlanta State Park sits on the fertile shores of Wright Patman Lake—a reservoir created in 1953 for flood control and water conservation. Before modern development, this area was known as a settlement for Indigenous tribes.

The park suffered extensive flooding in 2016 when Wright Patman Lake levels rose dramatically, submerging picnic areas and the amphitheater. With significant restoration efforts afterward, the park has since rebounded and offers a mix of camping, boating, and woodland tranquility.

Top Trails & Sites Visited
- ☐ Bobo's Ferry Trail (0.5 mi)
- ☐ Volksmarch Trail (0.7 mi)
- ☐ Arrowhead Trail (0.8 mi)
- ☐ Terrace Trail (0.3 mi)
- ☐ Hickory Hollow Nat. Trail (0.7 mi)
- ☐ White Oak Ridge Trail (1.2 mi)

Date of Visit: ____

Where did you stay? ____

Who were you with? ____

What did you do? ____

Favorite Memories? ____

____

____

State Park Stamp

Interesting Facts
- Atlanta SP covers 1,475 acres—one of the largest in East Texas.
- Offers full RV hookups and two public beaches on Wright Patman Lake.
- The park has 4.5 miles of hiking trails through loblolly pine forests.
- It includes a volleyball court, basketball court, horseshoe pits, and playground—great for families.
- Wildlife includes bald eagles, pine warblers, fox squirrels, and timber rattlesnakes.

Park Website

Park Maps

Visit the Texas Parks & Wildlife Department at tpwd.texas.gov

Caddo Lake State Park

245 Park Road 2, Karnack, TX 75661 - Hours: Open daily from 8:15 AM to 4:45 PM

2X3 photo

History

Caddo Lake State Park holds the distinction of being **Texas's first state park, dedicated in 1934**. Its origin aligns with broader conservation efforts, with initial infrastructure built by the Works Progress Administration.

The area was historically important to the Caddo tribe and became a steamboat hub in the 19th century. The state park preserves 484 acres of lush bald cypress swamp—such as through the iconic Saw Mill Pond—connected to Big Cypress Bayou, and celebrates a long history of ecological and cultural importance.

Top Trails & Sites Visited

☐ Caddo Forest Trail (0.7 mi)
☐ Pine Ridge Spur (0.2 mi)
☐ Pine Ridge Loop (0.8 mi)
☐ CCC Cut-through (0.2 mi)
☐ Saw Mill Pond Boardwalk
☐ Other: _________________________

Date of Visit: ____

Where did you stay? ____

Who were you with? ____

What did you do? ____

Favorite Memories? ____

____

Interesting Facts

- Home to 53 campsites with different hookup levels—including 8 full-hookup sites.
- Famed for alligator sightings, especially around Saw Mill Pond.
- The park hosts the annual Caddo Lake Bird Festival in spring.
- Historic cabins, built in the 1930s WPA/Civilian Conservation Corps era, are still in use.
- Fishing includes largemouth bass, crappie, and catfish—great for anglers of all ages.

State Park Stamp

Park Website

Park Maps

Visit the Texas Parks & Wildlife Department at tpwd.texas.gov

Daingerfield State Park

455 Park Road 17, Daingerfield, TX 75638 - Hours: Open daily from 6 AM to 10 PM

2X3 photo

History

Daingerfield State Park began as a private land deeded to Texas in 1935, and **opened in 1938** after infrastructure was built by Civilian Conservation Corps workers, notably Company 2891 and 1801. They constructed the park lodge, dammed to form Little Pine Lake, and replanted deforested areas.

Closed for renovation in 2011, the park upgraded facilities and campsites. Its design reflects classic CCC craftsmanship and Depression-era park development ethos.

Top Trails & Sites Visited

☐ Rustling Leaves Trail (2.4 mi)
☐ Mountain View Trail (0.8 mi)
☐ Historic Entry Sign
☐ Bridge and CCC dam
☐ Repurposed Boat House
☐ Other: _______________________

Date of Visit: ____

Where did you stay? ____

Who were you with? ____

What did you do? ____

Favorite Memories? ____

____

State Park Stamp

Interesting Facts

- The park includes cabin rentals, dorm-style lodges, and primitive campsites.
- The Rustling Leaves Trail circles Little Pine Lake for 2.4 miles.
- Canoes, kayaks, pedal boats, and paddleboards are available for rent onsite.
- The grounds feature an amphitheater used for park and community events.
- Wildlife includes beavers, pileated woodpeckers, painted buntings, and chain pickerel fish.

Park Website

Park Maps

Visit the Texas Parks & Wildlife Department at tpwd.texas.gov

Fort Boggy State Park

4994 TX-75 South, Centerville, TX 75833 - Hours: Open daily from 8 AM to Sunset

2X3 photo

History

Fort Boggy State Park **opened in 2001** and protects over 1,800 acres of forest, wetlands, and open water in East Texas. It's named after a nearby early 1800s frontier fort, though the exact fort location has not been found.

This quiet park was once part of a larger ranch and farmland system along the Boggy and Sullivan Creeks. Today, it serves as a serene escape for hikers, paddlers, and families seeking a peaceful natural setting. Its small lake, abundant wildlife, and easy trails make it ideal for low-key recreation.

Top Trails & Sites Visited

☐ Campbell Trail (1.17 mi)
☐ Leon Prairie Trail (0.41 mi)
☐ Lake Trail (1 mi)
☐ Tunnel Trail (0.37 mi)
☐ Other: _______________________
☐ Other: _______________________

Date of Visit: ____

Where did you stay? ____

Who were you with? ____

What did you do? ____

Favorite Memories? ____

Interesting Facts

- The lake is open to non-motorized boats only, creating a peaceful paddling and fishing experience.
- Boggy Slough is a unique East Texas wetland ecosystem with beavers, frogs, and herons.
- Trails cross wooded ridges, seasonal creeks, and lowland swamp areas.
- It's a favorite for school groups and homeschool nature field trips.
- The park is rarely crowded, even on weekends, making it a hidden gem.

State Park Stamp

Park Website

Park Maps

Visit the Texas Parks & Wildlife Department at tpwd.texas.gov

Lake Bob Sandlin State Park

341 State Park Road 2117, Pittsburg, TX 75686   -   Hours: Open daily from 8 AM to 10 PM

2X3 photo

History

Lake Bob Sandlin State Park **opened in 1987** on the northern edge of the Pineywoods. It borders a large reservoir created in 1977 by impounding Big Cypress Creek with the Fort Sherman Dam. The land was once home to Caddo people, and archaeological studies have uncovered pottery fragments and tools in the region.

The park is named for Bob Sandlin, a local civic leader who championed conservation efforts and helped secure funding for the dam project. The area now serves both as a wildlife refuge and a water recreation hub. It is known for its hardwood forests, seasonal color, and variety of fish that thrive in the cool, deep lake.

Top Trails & Sites Visited

☐ Dogwood Trail (1.7 mi)
☐ Lakeview Loop (0.6 mi)
☐ Brim Pond Trail (0.3 mi)
☐ Homestead Trail (0.4 mi)
☐ Fort Sherman Cemetery
☐ Other: _______________________

Date of Visit: ____

Where did you stay? ____

Who were you with? ____

What did you do? ____

Favorite Memories? ____

____

____

State Park Stamp

Interesting Facts

- Home to over 3.5 miles of multi-use trails through oak-hickory forests.
- One of the few Texas parks where white-tailed deer often graze near campsites.
- Anglers can catch hybrid striped bass, catfish, and crappie year-round.
- The park features a fishing pier, boat ramp, and fish cleaning station.
- Visitors in fall can see vibrant tree color changes uncommon in most of Texas.

Park Website

Park Maps

Visit the Texas Parks & Wildlife Department at tpwd.texas.gov

Lake Livingston State Park

300 Park Road 65, Livingston, TX 77351 - Hours: Open daily from 8 AM to 10 PM

2X3 photo

History

Lake Livingston State Park opened in 1977, a few years after the completion of the Lake Livingston Reservoir, which was created by damming the Trinity River in the late 1960s. The lake, one of the largest in Texas, was built to supply water to the Houston metropolitan area. The state park was designed as a recreational outlet to serve both locals and visitors, providing access to the massive reservoir while protecting a stretch of native Pineywoods and shoreline habitat.

The surrounding area, once home to several tribes including the Alabama and Coushatta tribes, became a logging and agriculture hub during the 19th and 20th centuries. The park now blends lakefront leisure with the natural heritage of East Texas.

Top Trails & Sites Visited

☐ Pineywoods Nature Trail (0.9 mi)
☐ Oak Flat Trail (0.6 mi)
☐ Hawthorn Trail (0.2 mi)
☐ Fó:Si Trail (0.5 mi)
☐ Trinity Trace (2.1 mi)
☐ Other:_________________________

Date of Visit: _______________________________________

Where did you stay? _______________________________________

Who were you with? _______________________________________

What did you do? _______________________________________

Favorite Memories? _______________________________________

____

Interesting Facts

- Lake Livingston is the second-largest lake entirely within Texas, spanning over 83,000 acres.
- The park has a boat ramp, fishing pier, and fish cleaning station for anglers.
- It's a top destination for catfish and white bass fishing year-round.
- You can rent paddle boards, kayaks, and bikes directly at the park.
- There's a nature center with exhibits about local wildlife and wetlands.

State Park Stamp

Park Website

Park Maps

Visit the Texas Parks & Wildlife Department at tpwd.texas.gov

Lake Tawakoni State Park

10822 FM 2475, Wills Point, TX 75169   -   Hours: Open daily from 6 AM to 10 PM

2X3 photo

History

Lake Tawakoni State Park **opened in 2002** on the western shore of the 37,879-acre Lake Tawakoni, which was created in 1960 by damming the Sabine River. The park preserves 376 acres of oak woodlands, grasslands, and shoreline in what was once farmland and open prairie. It serves as a refuge for birds and pollinators in the rapidly developing region east of Dallas.

The park is named after the Tawakoni people, a branch of the Wichita tribe. In 2007, it gained national attention when a massive communal spiderweb covered several acres of trail — drawing scientists and media from around the country.

Top Trails & Sites Visited

- ☐ Spring Point Trail (0.4 mi)
- ☐ Farkleberry Trail (0.5 mi)
- ☐ Red Oak Trail (0.4 mi)
- ☐ Spring Point Branch Trail (0.1 mi)
- ☐ White Deer Trail (0.4 mi)
- ☐ Other: _______________________

Date of Visit: _______________________________________

Where did you stay? _______________________________________

Who were you with? _______________________________________

What did you do? _______________________________________

Favorite Memories? _______________________________________

____

____

State Park Stamp

Interesting Facts

- The 2007 "mega spiderweb" covered over 200 yards of trail and trees — a rare natural phenomenon.
- The park has a designated Dark Sky viewing area, perfect for stargazing.
- Over 200 species of birds have been documented here, making it a favorite among birdwatchers.
- Shoreline access is great for kayaking and bank fishing — no boat required.
- It's one of the closest full-featured state parks to the Dallas–Fort Worth metroplex.

Park Website   Park Maps

Visit the Texas Parks & Wildlife Department at tpwd.texas.gov

Martin Creek Lake State Park

9515 County Road 2181D, Tatum, TX 75691   -   Hours: Open daily from 6 AM to 10 PM

2X3 photo

History

Opened in 1976, Martin Creek Lake State Park sits along the banks of its namesake reservoir, which was created in 1974 to provide cooling water for a nearby power plant. Despite the industrial roots of the lake, the surrounding land was preserved and developed into a scenic park that now supports fishing, birdwatching, and camping. The lake's warm water makes it a favorite for winter fishing, attracting both amateur anglers and professional tournaments.

Before development, the area was known for timber harvesting and small-scale farming. The park now balances human history with conservation. It offers peaceful shoreline, quiet forests, and varied aquatic life.

Top Trails & Sites Visited

- ☐ Harmony Hill Loop (1.5 mi)
- ☐ Island Trail (0.9 mi)
- ☐ Old Henderson Road Loop (1.2 mi)
- ☐ Pine Plantation
- ☐ Harmony Hill Cemetery
- ☐ Other: _______________________

Date of Visit: ____

Where did you stay? ____

Who were you with? ____

What did you do? ____

Favorite Memories? ____

Interesting Facts

- One of the best parks in Texas for winter bass fishing, thanks to warm lake water.
- Has a designated swimming area, rare in East Texas parks.
- The park rents out kayaks, canoes, and paddleboats seasonally.
- Home to several scenic lakefront campsites with tree canopy overhead.
- The lake attracts migratory waterfowl and wading birds, especially in cooler months.

State Park Stamp

Park Website

Park Maps

Martin Dies, Jr. State Park

634 Park Road 48 South, Jasper, TX 75951   -   Hours: Open daily from 8 AM to 10 PM

2X3 photo

History

Established in 1964 and named after state senator Martin Dies, Jr., this park was created to provide access to the newly constructed B.A. Steinhagen Reservoir, built by the U.S. Army Corps of Engineers for flood control and water supply.

The area borders the Big Thicket, a UNESCO Biosphere Reserve known for its astonishing ecological diversity. Early settlers used the Neches and Angelina rivers for logging and trade, and the surrounding lands have long been recognized for their unique biodiversity.

Today, the park's mission is dual: provide outdoor recreation and preserve the wild land corridor linking the Big Thicket to East Texas waterways.

Top Trails & Sites Visited

- ☐ Slough Trail (2.2 mi)
- ☐ Island Trail (0.8 mi)
- ☐ Wildlife Trail (1.4 mi)
- ☐ Whitetail Trail (0.7 mi)
- ☐ Forest Trail (1.0 mi)
- ☐ Other:_________________________

Date of Visit: ____

Where did you stay? ____

Who were you with? ____

What did you do? ____

Favorite Memories? ____

____

State Park Stamp

Interesting Facts

- The park has over 14 miles of hiking and biking trails, many of which wind through pine uplands and bayous.
- The park is a designated site on the Great Texas Wildlife Trails, making it a prime spot for birdwatchers.
- You can rent canoes and kayaks on-site — a rare amenity among Texas state parks.
- The park features two scenic camping loops (Hen House and Walnut Ridge), both offering shaded spots with lake views.

Park Website   Park Maps

Visit the Texas Parks & Wildlife Department at tpwd.texas.gov

Mission Tejas State Park

19343 State Highway 21 E, Grapeland, TX 75844   -   Hours: Open daily (no gate)

2X3 photo

History

Mission Tejas commemorates Mission San Francisco de los Tejas, the first Spanish mission in Texas founded in 1690. The mission quickly closed, but its legacy led locals to conserve the site in **1934**. They invited the CCC (Company 888) to construct park facilities including a replica mission chapel, trails, and picnic structures.

The community also donated the Rice Family Log Home (dating from 1828), believed to be one of the oldest structures in Houston County. In 1957, management transitioned from Texas Forest Service to TPWD, and today the park preserves historic, cultural, and ecological heritage deep in the Pineywoods.

Top Trails & Sites Visited

☐ Karl Lovett Trail (0.5 mi)
☐ Olen Matchett Trail (0.5 mi)
☐ Nabedache Loop (1.1 mi)
☐ CCC Bathtub Trail (0.1 mi)
☐ Rice Family Log Home
☐ Other: _______________________

Date of Visit: ____

Where did you stay? ____

Who were you with? ____

What did you do? ____

Favorite Memories? ____

____

Interesting Facts

- Contains over 8.5 miles of trails, including the historic Nabedache Loop following El Camino Real ruts.
- The Rice Family Log Home still has original wallpaper from the 1890s at one spot inside.
- The park has a reconstruction of CCC-era stone bathtubs used by workers.
- Dogwoods bloom in late March, turning the forest into a show of white and pink each spring.
- It's home to a raised CCC-built fire watch tower, offering a scenic overlook of Pineywoods.

State Park Stamp

Park Website

Park Maps

Visit the Texas Parks & Wildlife Department at tpwd.texas.gov

Tyler State Park

789 Park Road 16, Tyler, TX 75706   -   Hours: Open daily from 8 AM to 10 PM

2X3 photo

History

Tyler State Park was built during the Great Depression by the Civilian Conservation Corps (CCC) and **officially opened in 1939**. The CCC constructed the park's 64-acre lake, stone retaining walls, trails, and the original group pavilions — many of which are still used today. The area was heavily logged before the 1930s, and the park's creation included reforestation efforts to restore the native Pineywoods ecosystem.

This park stands as one of the best-preserved CCC parks in Texas, combining historical craftsmanship with natural beauty. It quickly became a favorite weekend retreat for East Texans and remains popular year-round thanks to its elevation, forest shade, and lake recreation.

Top Trails & Sites Visited

☐ Lakeshore Trail (2.1 mi)
☐ Whispering Pines Trail (1.0 mi)
☐ Blackjack Nature Trail (0.3 mi)
☐ CCC Overlook
☐ CCC Rock Dam
☐ Other: _______________________

Date of Visit: ____

Where did you stay? ____

Who were you with? ____

What did you do? ____

Favorite Memories? ____

____

State Park Stamp

Interesting Facts

- The park's stonework, cabins, and trails were hand-built by CCC Company 2888.
- Tyler State Park Lake is spring-fed and known for its clear, cool water.
- The Whispering Pines Trail is one of the oldest CCC-built trails in the state park system.
- Offers boat, kayak, and paddleboard rentals from a seasonal boathouse.
- Fall and early spring offer some of the best foliage viewing in East Texas.

Park Website

Park Maps

Visit the Texas Parks & Wildlife Department at tpwd.texas.gov

Village Creek State Park

8854 Park Road 74, Lumberton, TX 77657   -   Hours: Open daily from 8 AM to 10 PM

2X3 photo

History

Village Creek State Park, **established in 1994,** protects a rare piece of the Big Thicket ecosystem, one of the most biologically diverse areas in North America. Before becoming a state park, the land was part of the larger Big Thicket area.

The creek itself, a free-flowing tributary of the Neches River, was historically a water source and travel route for Native American tribes and later settlers. In the 20th century, logging and industrial activity threatened the region, leading to concerted efforts by state and federal conservationists to protect these remaining wild lands. Village Creek State Park was created to serve as a publicly accessible preserve and gateway to the wonders of the Big Thicket.

Top Trails & Sites Visited

- ☐ Village Slough Inner loop (0.5 mi)
- ☐ Water Oak Trail (2.4 mi)
- ☐ River Birch Trail (0.2 mi)
- ☐ Village Creek Trail (2.2 mi)
- ☐ Tupelo Trail (0.8 mi)
- ☐ Other:_____________________

Date of Visit: ____

Where did you stay? ____

Who were you with? ____

What did you do? ____

Favorite Memories? ____

____

Interesting Facts

- Village Creek is one of the few free-flowing creeks left in Texas.
- The park is part of the larger Big Thicket National Preserve ecosystem.
- You can spot carnivorous plants, like pitcher plants, in some parts of the park.
- Popular for paddling and canoeing, especially along the Village Creek Paddling Trail.
- Contains sandy white "beaches" along the creek — rare in East Texas woodlands.

State Park Stamp

Park Website   Park Maps

Visit the Texas Parks & Wildlife Department at tpwd.texas.gov

Bastrop State Park

100 Park Road 1A, Bastrop, TX 78602   -   Hours: Open daily from 6 AM to 10 PM

2X3 photo

History

Bastrop State Park **opened in 1937** and is one of Texas's most historic and beloved parks. It was developed by the Civilian Conservation Corps (CCC) during the Great Depression and features striking stone structures, bridges, and facilities built with native materials.

The park was once home to the "Lost Pines", an isolated forest of loblolly pine trees separated by over 100 miles from the Pineywoods of East Texas. In 2011, a devastating wildfire destroyed over 90% of the forest. Since then, TPWD has led major restoration and reforestation efforts to revive the unique ecosystem.

Top Trails & Sites Visited

- ☐ Post Oak Spur (0.5 mi)
- ☐ Piney Hill Spur (0.3 mi)
- ☐ Farkleberry Spur (0.4 mi)
- ☐ Scenic Overlook Trail (1.7 mi)
- ☐ Historic Water Fountain
- ☐ Other: _______________________

Date of Visit: ____

Where did you stay? ____

Who were you with? ____

What did you do? ____

Favorite Memories? ____

____

State Park Stamp

Interesting Facts

- The Lost Pines ecosystem is unique to this region of Texas.
- The 2011 Bastrop Complex Fire was one of the most destructive wildfires in Texas history.
- CCC structures like the refectory and stone cabins are still in use today.
- You can drive Park Road 1C, which connects Bastrop and Buescher State Parks.
- Bastrop State Park is listed on the National Register of Historic Places.

Park Website

Park Maps

Visit the Texas Parks & Wildlife Department at tpwd.texas.gov

Buescher State Park

100 Park Road 1E, Smithville, TX 78957   -   Hours: Open daily from 6 AM to 10 PM

2X3 photo

History

Buescher State Park **opened in 1940** and, like its sister park Bastrop, was developed by the Civilian Conservation Corps (CCC). The park protects a section of the Lost Pines, a remnant pine forest unique to this part of Texas. Much of the landscape was historically used for timber and grazing until the CCC transformed it into a scenic public space.

Although it's smaller and quieter than Bastrop, Buescher offers serene woodlands, a small fishing lake, and access to the scenic Park Road 1C, which connects the two parks. Buescher was also affected by the 2011 wildfire, but replanting efforts have helped restore its lush, peaceful feel.

Top Trails & Sites Visited

- ☐ Winding Woodland Trail (1.5 mi)
- ☐ Barred Owl Path (0.1 mi)
- ☐ Pine Gulch Trail (4 mi)
- ☐ CCC Crossover (0.1 mi)
- ☐ Big Tree Retreat (0.03 mi)
- ☐ Other: ___________________

Date of Visit: ____

Where did you stay? ____

Who were you with? ____

What did you do? ____

Favorite Memories? ____

____

Interesting Facts

- The park features a small, spring-fed lake popular for fishing and canoeing.
- It's connected to Bastrop State Park via the 12-mile scenic Park Road 1C, great for cycling.
- Rustic stone picnic shelters and a scenic overlook were built by the CCC.
- Buescher has been part of large pine ecosystem recovery efforts since 2011.
- It's a favorite for quiet retreats, with fewer crowds than nearby Bastrop.

State Park Stamp

Park Website

Park Maps

Visit the Texas Parks & Wildlife Department at tpwd.texas.gov

Fort Parker State Park

194 Park Road 28, Mexia, TX 76667 - Hours: Open daily from 8 AM to 5 PM

2X3 photo

History

Fort Parker State Park **opened in 1941** and preserves a unique combination of Texas frontier history and natural beauty. Built by the Civilian Conservation Corps (CCC), the park includes both modern recreational facilities and a reconstructed version of Old Fort Parker, the original 1830s stockade famous for the 1836 raid and kidnapping of Cynthia Ann Parker.

The park lies along the Navasota River and includes Lake Fort Parker, a small reservoir created for fishing, paddling, and wildlife watching. The blend of prairie, forest, and river bottom makes this a peaceful spot for outdoor lovers and history buffs alike.

Top Trails & Sites Visited

☐ Springfield Trail (1.8 mi)
☐ River Loop (0.9 mi)
☐ Bur Oak Trail (0.5 mi)
☐ Navasota River Trail (2.5 mi)
☐ Springfield Cemetery
☐ Other: ______________________

Date of Visit: ____

Where did you stay? _______________________________________

Who were you with? _______________________________________

What did you do? ____

Favorite Memories? _______________________________________

____

State Park Stamp

Interesting Facts

- The park is home to Old Fort Parker, a reconstructed fort managed separately and available for tours.
- You can paddle the Limestone Bluffs Paddling Trail, a scenic 5.3-mile loop along the Navasota River.
- CCC-built picnic shelters, cabins, and a group hall still stand and are used today.
- Fort Parker honors the story of Cynthia Ann Parker, mother of Comanche chief Quanah Parker.
- The park includes historic cemeteries and interpretive signs about frontier life.

Park Website

Park Maps

Visit the Texas Parks & Wildlife Department at tpwd.texas.gov

Huntsville State Park

565 Park Rd 40 W, Huntsville, TX 77340   -   Hours: Open daily from 8 AM to 10 PM

2X3 photo

History

Huntsville State Park was developed in the late 1930s and early 1940s during the Great Depression, as part of a nationwide effort by the Civilian Conservation Corps (CCC) to provide jobs and create public recreational areas. CCC Company, composed of African American veterans, built the park's roads, trails, bridges, and picnic shelters by hand.

Set in the Pineywoods of East Texas, the park's original design emphasized harmony with nature, a hallmark of CCC craftsmanship. Today, Huntsville State Park stands as a tribute to their labor and vision. It's also located near the Sam Houston National Forest — home to Sam Houston himself, adding a broader layer of Texas historical connection.

Top Trails & Sites Visited

- ☐ Loblolly Trail (0.2 mi)
- ☐ Coloneh Trail (0.8 mi)
- ☐ Prairie Branch Loop (1.5 mi)
- ☐ Dogwood Trail (1.8 mi)
- ☐ Chinquapin Trail (6.9 mi)
- ☐ Other:_________________________

Date of Visit: ____

Where did you stay? ____

Who were you with? ____

What did you do? ____

Favorite Memories? ____

____

Interesting Facts

- Includes the scenic Triple C Trail, which creates a small wetland by partially damming a creek.
- Home to bald eagles, pileated woodpeckers, and alligators in park waterways.
- The CCC-built lodge and culverts are listed as historic sites.
- Popular for first-day hikes and group events, reflecting active park programming.

Park Website   Park Maps

Visit the Texas Parks & Wildlife Department at tpwd.texas.gov

State Park Stamp

Sheldon Lake State Park

14140 Garrett Rd, Houston, TX 77044   -   Hours: Open daily from 8 AM to 5 PM

2X3 photo

History

Originally constructed as a fish hatchery and water reservoir in the 1940s, Sheldon Lake played a vital role during World War II by supplying water to nearby shipyards. After the war, the area was repurposed for conservation and recreation, and **in 1952, the reservoir opened for public fishing.** The land surrounding it gradually transitioned into a full-fledged state park with the establishment of the Environmental Learning Center in 2003.

Today, Sheldon Lake is a living laboratory for ecological education, offering an immersive outdoor experience just 15 minutes from downtown Houston. It emphasizes urban conservation, wetland restoration, and environmental science programs for schools and families.

Top Trails & Sites Visited

- ☐ Pond Loop Trail (0.6 mi)
- ☐ Prairie Trail (0.6 mi)
- ☐ Wetland Loop (0.2 mi)
- ☐ Swamp Rabbit Trail (0.4 mi)
- ☐ Observation Tower
- ☐ Other:_______________________

Date of Visit: _______________________

Where did you stay? _______________________

Who were you with? _______________________

What did you do? _______________________

Favorite Memories? _______________________

State Park Stamp

Interesting Facts

- The 250-foot observation tower offers sweeping views of downtown Houston and the wetlands.
- Home to over 250 species of birds, including herons, roseate spoonbills, and hawks.
- Features interactive wetlands boardwalks that pass through native plant restoration zones.
- Offers fishing access for people with disabilities, plus loaner poles for kids.
- Frequently hosts free ranger programs and school field trips on wildlife and conservation.

Park Website

Park Maps

Visit the Texas Parks & Wildlife Department at tpwd.texas.gov

Bentsen-Rio Grande Valley State Park

2800 South Bentsen Palm Drive, Mission, TX 78572 - Hours: Open daily from 7 AM to 10 PM

2X3 photo

History

Established in 1944, Bentsen-Rio Grande Valley State Park is one of Texas' oldest birding parks and serves as the headquarters of the World Birding Center. Located on the border with Mexico, this 760-acre preserve protects one of the last remaining riparian woodlands along the Rio Grande.

Once part of the Bentsen family ranch, the land was donated to the state with the condition that it be preserved for wildlife. Today, it is internationally renowned for birding and wildlife photography and plays a critical role in habitat conservation for endangered species and neotropical migrants.

Top Trails & Sites Visited

☐ Hawk Tower (0.2 mi)
☐ Rio Grande Trail (1.8 mi)
☐ Acacia Loop (0.4 mi)
☐ Resaca Vieja Trail (1.4 mi)
☐ Other: _______________________
☐ Other: _______________________

Date of Visit: ____

Where did you stay? ____

Who were you with? ____

What did you do? ____

Favorite Memories? ____

____

____

Interesting Facts

- The park is a no-car zone beyond headquarters — it's explored by foot, bike, or park tram.
- It has over seven bird blinds, water features, and butterfly gardens for wildlife viewing.
- Visitors may spot rare species like the green jay, gray hawk, chachalaca, or Altamira oriole.
- The resaca system (former Rio Grande channel) creates seasonal wetlands in the park.
- It's a prime site for birding festivals, workshops, and ranger-led hikes throughout the year.

State Park Stamp

Park Website

Park Maps

Choke Canyon State Park

358 Recreation Road 8, Calliham, TX 78007 – Hours: Open daily from 6 AM to 10 PM

2X3 photo

History

Choke Canyon State Park was **established in 1986** after the construction of Choke Canyon Reservoir by the U.S. Bureau of Reclamation. The lake was created for water supply and flood control, but it quickly became a haven for outdoor recreation.

The park includes two units: the larger Calliham Unit and the smaller South Shore Unit (day-use only). Located in the brush country of South Texas, the park preserves a mix of mesquite, blackbrush, and prickly pear — ideal habitat for wildlife like javelinas, deer, wild turkeys, and American alligators. The area is also a hotspot for birdwatching along migratory flyways.

Top Trails & Sites Visited

- ☐ Bird Trail (0.5 mi)
- ☐ Other: _________________________
- ☐ Other: _________________________
- ☐ Other: _________________________
- ☐ Other: _________________________
- ☐ Other: _________________________
- ☐ Other: _________________________

Date of Visit: ____

Where did you stay? ______________________________________

Who were you with? ______________________________________

What did you do? ____

Favorite Memories? ______________________________________

____

State Park Stamp

Interesting Facts

- The park is home to a population of wild alligators — often spotted in and around the lake.
- Birders can spot over 200 species, including crested caracaras and green jays.
- Choke Canyon Reservoir covers over 25,000 acres when full.
- The 75-person group hall and lodge can be reserved for large events.
- The lake is known for trophy bass and catfish, popular with anglers statewide.

Park Website   Park Maps

Visit the Texas Parks & Wildlife Department at tpwd.texas.gov

Estero Llano Grande State Park

3301 S. FM 1015, Weslaco, TX 78596 – Hours: Open daily from 8 AM to 5 PM

2X3 photo

History

Estero Llano Grande State Park **opened in 2006** and serves as the heart of the World Birding Center network in the Lower Rio Grande Valley. The park was created from former agricultural land and citrus groves, which were transformed into a mosaic of wetlands, ponds, woodlands, and thorn scrub.

The name "Estero Llano Grande" refers to a historic oxbow lake system in the region. TPWD and its partners restored the landscape to create critical habitat for birds and butterflies, helping reverse habitat loss in this biologically rich area. The park is a beloved destination for birders, photographers, and nature lovers.

Top Trails & Sites Visited

- ☐ Orchard Trail (0.42 mi)
- ☐ Wader's Trail (1.16 mi)
- ☐ Alligator Lake Trail (0.1 mi)
- ☐ Tropical Trail (0.74 mi)
- ☐ Alligator Lake
- ☐ Other: _______________________

Date of Visit: ____

Where did you stay? ____

Who were you with? ____

What did you do? ____

Favorite Memories? ____

____

____

Interesting Facts

- The park has extensive boardwalks and observation decks over wetland ponds.
- It's one of the top birding sites in the U.S., with sightings of rarities like the common pauraque, groove-billed ani, and tropical kingbird.
- Alligator Pond hosts a small population of resident gators — visible from a safe distance.
- Interpretive programs include owl prowls, butterfly walks, and seasonal night hikes.

State Park Stamp

Park Website

Park Maps

Visit the Texas Parks & Wildlife Department at tpwd.texas.gov

Falcon State Park

146 Park Rd 46, Falcon Heights, TX 78545 - Hours: Open daily from 7 AM to 10 PM

2X3 photo

History

Falcon State Park was **established in the 1960s** after the creation of Falcon International Reservoir, a massive lake formed by damming the Rio Grande in 1954. The park lies on the U.S.–Mexico border and was designed to provide recreation access to the reservoir, which serves as a vital water source for both countries.

The landscape consists of South Texas desert brush, mesquite, and thorny scrubland — and it's one of the quietest and least developed state parks, perfect for solitude, wildlife watching, and fishing. The park is known for its dramatic sunsets, winter birding, and peaceful waterfront campsites.

Top Trails & Sites Visited

☐ Hiking Trail Loop (2.6 mi)
☐ Butterfly Garden
☐ Other: _______________________
☐ Other: _______________________
☐ Other: _______________________
☐ Other: _______________________

Date of Visit: ____

Where did you stay? ____

Who were you with? ____

What did you do? ____

Favorite Memories? ____

____

State Park Stamp

Interesting Facts

- The park is popular among "Winter Texans" for its mild climate and birding.
- You can see Mexico across the lake from many spots in the park.
- Falcon Lake is shared between the U.S. and Mexico — you'll need a special permit to boat on both sides.
- Campgrounds are often visited by javelinas, roadrunners, and green jays.
- A remote feel and minimal development make it ideal for stargazing and photography.

Park Website

Park Maps

Visit the Texas Parks & Wildlife Department at tpwd.texas.gov

Goliad State Park & Historic Site

108 Park Road 6, Goliad, TX 77963   -   Hours: Open daily from 8 AM to 5 PM

2X3 photo

History

Goliad State Park & Historic Site preserves a key location in Texas Revolution history. The park is home to the beautifully reconstructed Mission Espíritu Santo, a Spanish mission originally founded in 1749 to convert and educate native Aranama peoples.

The park also sits near the site of the Goliad Massacre during the Texas Revolution, where hundreds of Texian soldiers were executed under Mexican orders — an event that became a rallying cry alongside "Remember the Alamo." Today, the park offers a rare blend of Spanish colonial architecture, Revolutionary War history, and riverfront camping.

Top Trails & Sites Visited

- ☐ Angel of Goliad Trail (2.5 mi)
- ☐ San Antonio River Trail (1 mi)
- ☐ Mission Espíritu Santo
- ☐ Aranama Trail (0.25 mi)
- ☐ Other: _______________________________
- ☐ Other: _______________________________

Date of Visit: ____

Where did you stay? ____

Who were you with? ____

What did you do? ____

Favorite Memories? ____

____

Interesting Facts

- Mission Espíritu Santo is one of the most complete mission reconstructions in the state.
- You can visit the nearby Presidio La Bahía and Fannin Memorial Monument, both historically tied to the 1836 massacre.
- The park is located along the San Antonio River and is part of the Goliad Paddling Trail.
- CCC workers in the 1930s restored the mission and built many of the park's original facilities.

State Park Stamp

Park Website

Park Maps

Visit the Texas Parks & Wildlife Department at tpwd.texas.gov

Lake Casa Blanca International State Park

5102 Bob Bullock Loop, Laredo, TX 78041 - Hours: Open daily from 7 AM to 10 PM

2X3 photo

History

Lake Casa Blanca International State Park **opened in 1991** and was developed around a reservoir originally built in the 1950s by the U.S. Bureau of Reclamation. The lake was designed for flood control and recreation in the rapidly growing Laredo area.

This park is a true urban oasis, sitting right on the city's east side but offering green space, lake access, and trails for locals and travelers alike. Though not as remote as other South Texas parks, it provides an easy escape into nature for boating, hiking, picnicking, and wildlife watching — all with city convenience.

Top Trails & Sites Visited

- ☐ Roadrunner Trail (1.0 mi)
- ☐ Mesquite Bend Trail (1.5 mi loop)
- ☐ Osprey Hill Loop (0.8 mi)
- ☐ White-Tail Loop (1.0 mi)
- ☐ Old Museum
- ☐ Other: _______________________

Date of Visit: _______________________

Where did you stay? _______________________

Who were you with? _______________________

What did you do? _______________________

Favorite Memories? _______________________

State Park Stamp

Interesting Facts

- It's one of only a few "International" State Parks, located near the U.S.–Mexico border.
- The park offers paddleboard and kayak rentals, perfect for calm days on the lake.
- Visitors regularly spot migratory birds and waterfowl, especially in spring and fall.
- The borderland culture of Laredo is reflected in the park's design and local events.
- It's a favorite for school field trips and urban outdoor education programs.

Park Website   Park Maps

Visit the Texas Parks & Wildlife Department at tpwd.texas.gov

Lake Corpus Christi State Park

23194 Park Road 25, Mathis, TX 78368   -   Hours: Open daily from 6 AM to 10 PM

2X3 photo

History

Lake Corpus Christi State Park was **developed in the 1930s** through the efforts of the Civilian Conservation Corps (CCC), which built many of the park's original structures. The park sits on the northeastern shore of Lake Corpus Christi, a reservoir created in 1935 when the Wesley Seale Dam was built on the Nueces River.

The park was created to provide recreation opportunities for nearby communities and preserve native brushland and lakeshore habitat. Today, the park is popular for boating, fishing, camping, and swimming, and it continues to honor its CCC roots through preserved stone structures.

Top Trails & Sites Visited

- ☐ Catfish Point Trail
- ☐ Longhorn Trail
- ☐ Kiskadee Trail
- ☐ CCC Refectory
- ☐ Other: _______________________
- ☐ Other: _______________________

Date of Visit: ____

Where did you stay? ____

Who were you with? ____

What did you do? ____

Favorite Memories? ____

____

____

Interesting Facts

- The lake spans over 21,000 acres — making it a favorite for power boating and jet skiing.
- The park has several CCC-built picnic shelters and group halls, some restored.
- Birders may spot green jays, great kiskadees, and herons along the lakeshore.
- The park offers paddleboard and kayak rentals during peak seasons.
- Lake Corpus Christi is stocked with catfish, bass, and crappie year-round.

State Park Stamp

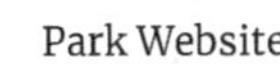

Park Website   Park Maps

Mustang Island State Park

9394 TX-361, Corpus Christi, TX 78418- Hours: Open daily from 7 AM to 10 PM

2X3 photo

History

Mustang Island was named after the wild mustangs that once roamed the island's dunes. The state acquired the land in the 1970s and **officially opened the park in 1979** to protect its coastal barrier island habitat and provide public access to the Gulf of Mexico.

For centuries, the island was a vital part of indigenous travel routes and later served as a pirate hideout, cattle range, and shipping point. Today, it is cherished for its natural beaches, bird migration paths, and surf friendly waters.

Top Trails & Sites Visited

- ☐ Beachfront Walk
- ☐ Paddling Trail
- ☐ Birding Areas
- ☐ Dune Exploration
- ☐ Fishing Jetty
- ☐ Other: _______________________

Date of Visit: _______________________________

Where did you stay? _______________________________

Who were you with? _______________________________

What did you do? _______________________________

Favorite Memories? _______________________________

____

State Park Stamp

Interesting Facts

- The park features 5 miles of uninterrupted beachfront for swimming, fishing, and sunbathing.
- It lies along the Central Flyway, making it ideal for birdwatching during migrations.
- You can camp right on the beach, just steps from the surf.
- Sea turtles and dolphins are often spotted offshore, especially in summer.
- The park is a launch point for the Mustang Island Paddling Trail, part of the Texas Paddling Trail system.

Park Website

Park Maps

Visit the Texas Parks & Wildlife Department at tpwd.texas.gov

"""

Resaca de la Palma State Park

1000 New Carmen Ave, Brownsville, TX 78521 – Hours: Open daily from 8 AM to 5 PM

2X3 photo

History

Resaca de la Palma State Park **opened in 2008** as part of the World Birding Center network and is one of the newest additions to the Texas State Parks system. Located within the city limits of Brownsville, the park preserves over 1,200 acres of restored native habitat along a former resaca — an ancient oxbow of the Rio Grande.

The park's name means "palm oxbow," reflecting the area's tropical feel and dense brush. Once farmland and citrus groves, this land has been reclaimed as a vital habitat for endangered birds, butterflies, and other wildlife.

Top Trails & Sites Visited

☐ Kiskadee Trail (0.06 mi)
☐ North Mexican Olive Trail (0.4 mi)
☐ Hog Trail (0.2 mi)
☐ Mexican Olive Trail (0.3 mi)
☐ Other: _______________________
☐ Other: _______________________

Date of Visit: ____

Where did you stay? ____

Who were you with? ____

What did you do? ____

Favorite Memories? ____

____

____

Interesting Facts

- It has one of the longest uninterrupted resaca systems in South Texas.
- The park features ADA-accessible trails and wildlife blinds, ideal for all ages.
- Over 300 bird species have been documented here, including groove-billed anis and ringed kingfishers.
- It's a hotspot for butterfly watchers, with dozens of tropical and subtropical species.
- You can borrow binoculars, bikes, or birding backpacks from the visitor center.

State Park Stamp

Park Website

Park Maps

Visit the Texas Parks & Wildlife Department at tpwd.texas.gov

Albert & Bessie Kronkosky State Natural Area

7690 TX-46, Boerne, TX 78006 - Hours: Open daily from 8 AM to 10 PM

2X3 photo

History

This 3,800-acre property was donated to the state in 2011 by the estate of Albert and Bessie Kronkosky, long-time Hill Country ranch owners. It was originally known as the Circle K Ranch, located on the western edge of the Edwards Plateau — a region known for steep canyons, limestone hills, and diverse wildlife.

The Kronkoskys left the land to Texas Parks & Wildlife to be preserved in its natural state, and the park was officially designated as a State Natural Area. Since then, TPWD has worked to survey rare species, restore habitat, and plan low-impact recreational opportunities that will eventually include hiking, nature study, and guided tours. The Park opened ____________________.

Top Trails & Sites Visited

☐
☐
☐
☐
☐ Other: ____________________
☐ Other: ____________________

Date of Visit: ____________________

Where did you stay? ____________________

Who were you with? ____________________

What did you do? ____________________

Favorite Memories? ____________________

State Park Stamp

Interesting Facts

- It sits within a biological transition zone, home to both Hill Country and South Texas species.
- Several rare or endangered species have been documented here, including the golden-cheeked warbler and Tobusch fishhook cactus.
- The landscape features spring-fed canyons, caves, and dense oak-juniper woodlands.
- The park is being developed as a low-impact natural area, with no traditional RV or tent camping planned.

Park Website

Park Maps

Visit the Texas Parks & Wildlife Department at tpwd.texas.gov

Bear Creek State Park

Hours: Open daily from _______ to _______

2X3 photo

History

Bear Creek State Park is Texas' newest addition to the state park system, announced in 2025 when the state purchased more than 1,700 acres in Uvalde County. The property lies less than a mile from the well-loved Garner State Park and is part of a long-term vision to expand outdoor spaces for future generations.

Rolling hills, spring-fed creeks, and dramatic canyon views reflect the beauty of the Hill Country, while historic ranch lands hint at its cultural past. Though still closed to the public, the park will undergo years of planning and restoration before welcoming visitors, ensuring its rivers, ridges, and wildlife remain protected.

Top Trails & Sites Visited

☐ Other:_____________________
☐ Other:_____________________
☐ Other:_____________________
☐ Other:_____________________
☐ Other:_____________________

Date of Visit: ____

Where did you stay? ____

Who were you with? ____

What did you do? ____

Favorite Memories? ____

____

____

Interesting Facts

- The land was acquired with support from the Centennial Parks Conservation Fund.
- Streams from Bear Creek, Spring Creek, and the Frio River cross through the property, making it a rare site with multiple waterways.
- Scenic ridges provide sweeping views, including sightlines to Old Baldy, a landmark at nearby Garner State Park.
- The area provides habitat for sensitive Hill Country wildlife.
- With minimal development around it, the park offers exceptional dark skies, ideal for future camping and stargazing opportunities.

State Park Stamp

Blanco State Park

101 Park Road 23, Blanco, TX 78606 - Hours: Open daily from 8 AM to 10 PM

2X3 photo

History

Established in 1934, Blanco State Park is one of the original parks developed by the Civilian Conservation Corps (CCC). Located along a scenic mile of the Blanco River, the CCC constructed stone picnic tables, a pavilion, restrooms, and a low-water dam that still stands today. The park was created during the Great Depression to promote jobs, conservation, and recreation in the Texas Hill Country.

Blanco's proximity to the historic town square — just a short walk from the park — adds to its charm and accessibility. Over time, it's become a beloved summer spot for tubing, swimming, and riverside family gatherings.

Top Trails & Sites Visited

☐ Caswell Nature Trail (0.8 mi)
☐ Pumphouse Trail (0.3 mi)
☐ The Falls
☐ CCC Stone Dam
☐ Other: _______________________
☐ Other: _______________________

Date of Visit: ____

Where did you stay? _______________________________________

Who were you with? _______________________________________

What did you do? ____

Favorite Memories? _______________________________________

____

____

State Park Stamp

Interesting Facts

- The park includes a CCC-built dam that creates a calm wading pool downstream.
- Visitors can tube, kayak, or paddleboard in the river depending on flow conditions.
- Blanco River water levels fluctuate naturally, creating a different experience with each visit.
- The park has accessible fishing piers and a stocked section of river (no license required within park limits).
- A small herd of white-tailed deer is commonly spotted near campsites at dawn and dusk.

Park Website

Park Maps

Visit the Texas Parks & Wildlife Department at tpwd.texas.gov

Colorado Bend State Park

2236 Park Hill Dr, Bend, TX 76824 – Hours: Open daily from 6 AM to 10 PM

2X3 photo

History

Once part of the sprawling Lemons Ranch, Colorado Bend became a **state park in 1987 and opened to the public in 1989**. For decades, the rugged canyons and wild riverbanks of this stretch of the Colorado River were known mostly to ranchers, anglers, and adventurous spelunkers.

The land features dramatic karst topography — including caves, springs, sinkholes, and waterfalls — shaped by millennia of underground water flow. Today, the park preserves over 5,300 acres of Hill Country wilderness and provides access to one of the most photographed waterfalls in Texas: Gorman Falls.

Top Trails & Sites Visited

- ☐ Gorman Springs Trail (0.5 mi)
- ☐ Gorman Falls Trail (1.5 mi)
- ☐ Spicewood Springs Trail (1.3 mi)
- ☐ Gorman Falls
- ☐ Other: _______________________
- ☐ Other: _______________________

Date of Visit: ____

Where did you stay? ____

Who were you with? ____

What did you do? ____

Favorite Memories? ____

____

Interesting Facts

- The park protects over 400 caves, many of which are closed to the public for conservation.
- Gorman Falls, at 70 feet tall, is one of Texas' tallest and most iconic waterfalls.
- Colorado Bend is home to endangered golden-cheeked warblers and cave-dwelling invertebrates.
- The Spicewood Springs trail features multiple creek crossings and natural swimming holes.
- It's one of the few state parks that offers guided wild cave tours.

State Park Stamp

Park Website

Park Maps

Enchanted Rock State Natural Area

16710 Ranch Rd 965, Fredericksburg, TX 78624 - Hours: Open daily from 6:30 AM to 10 PM

2X3 photo

History

Enchanted Rock is a massive pink granite dome rising 425 feet above the surrounding Hill Country, and part of a much larger underground batholith estimated to be over 1 billion years old. The area has long been considered sacred by Indigenous peoples, including the Tonkawa, Apache, and Comanche, who believed the dome was inhabited by spirits.

The site became a **protected natural area in 1978** and has since become one of Texas's premier hiking destinations. The park protects over 1,600 acres of rugged terrain, rare plants, and panoramic views of Central Texas — while preserving the legend and mystique of the "enchanted" rock.

Top Trails & Sites Visited

- ☐ Summit Trail (0.8 mi)
- ☐ Interpretive Loop (0.4 mi)
- ☐ Base Trail (0.9 mi)
- ☐ Enchanted Rock Summit
- ☐ Little Rock
- ☐ Other: ________________________

Date of Visit: ________________________

Where did you stay? ________________________

Who were you with? ________________________

What did you do? ________________________

Favorite Memories? ________________________

____

____

State Park Stamp

Interesting Facts

- On hot days, the rock "sings" as it cools, due to the granite cracking — giving rise to its mystical reputation.
- The dome is part of the Llano Uplift, a geologic formation over 1 billion years old.
- The summit offers 360-degree views of Hill Country valleys, ridges, and cedar breaks.
- Over 11 miles of trails loop around granite boulders, canyons, and creeks.
- It's a hotspot for rock climbing, stargazing, and birding.

Park Website   Park Maps

Visit the Texas Parks & Wildlife Department at tpwd.texas.gov

Garner State Park

234 RR 1050, Concan, TX 78838 – Hours: Open daily from 8 AM to 10 PM

2X3 photo

History

Garner State Park, **established in 1941**, is named after John Nance Garner, the 32nd Vice President of the United States, who was born in Uvalde County. The park was developed during the Great Depression by the Civilian Conservation Corps (CCC), whose craftsmanship is still evident in the park's stonework and pavilions.

Garner is one of the most popular state parks in Texas, beloved for its scenic beauty along the Frio River, where visitors enjoy swimming, tubing, hiking, and live music events in the summer.

Top Trails & Sites Visited

- ☐ Old Entrance Road (0.8 mi)
- ☐ Blinn River Trail (0.5 mi)
- ☐ Frio Canyon Trail (2.9 mi)
- ☐ Crystal Cave
- ☐ Painted Rock Overlook
- ☐ Other: _______________________

Date of Visit: _______________________

Where did you stay? _______________________

Who were you with? _______________________

What did you do? _______________________

Favorite Memories? _______________________

____

____

Interesting Facts

- The CCC constructed many of the park's iconic structures, including the dance pavilion, which hosts the famous summer dance series.
- Garner State Park is home to the "Texas State Cradle of Texas Music" during its summer events, attracting visitors with live country and folk music.
- It boasts a scenic overlook called "The Overlook," providing panoramic views of the Frio River valley.
- Nighttime at the park features popular stargazing opportunities due to its relatively low light pollution.

State Park Stamp

Park Website   Park Maps

Guadalupe River State Park

3350 Park Road 31, Spring Branch, TX 78070 - Hours: Open daily from 8 AM to 10 PM

2X3 photo

History

Guadalupe River State Park was **opened in 1983** and encompasses over 1,700 acres along the beautiful Guadalupe River. The land was once part of the San Antonio and Aransas Pass Railway corridor and has a rich heritage tied to early settlers and ranchers in the region.

The park preserves the native Texas Hill Country ecosystem, including limestone bluffs, oak and cedar trees, and native wildlife. It's a favorite spot for fishing, tubing, hiking, and camping.

Top Trails & Sites Visited

☐ Oak Savannah Loop (0.5 mi)
☐ Cedar Sage River Trail (0.4 mi)
☐ Bald Cypress Trail (0.6 mi)
☐ Little Bluestem Loop (0.7 mi)
☐ Rust House
☐ Other: ___________________________

Date of Visit: ____

Where did you stay? ____

Who were you with? ____

What did you do? ____

Favorite Memories? ____

____

____

State Park Stamp

Interesting Facts

- The park's river section features calm stretches perfect for beginner tubing and swimming.
- Guadalupe River State Park hosts an annual Texas Native Plant Society event, promoting conservation.
- Over 11 miles of hiking trails wind through varied landscapes, including canyon and river habitats.
- It has a unique bat observation site where visitors can see Mexican free-tailed bats during summer evenings.
- The park is home to several historical CCC-era stone structures built in the 1930s.

Park Website

Park Maps

Visit the Texas Parks & Wildlife Department at tpwd.texas.gov

Inks Lake State Park

3630 Park Road 4 West, Burnet, TX 78611 - Hours: Open daily from 8 AM to 10 PM

2X3 photo

History

Inks Lake State Park **opened in 1950** after the construction of Inks Lake, one of the Highland Lakes formed by the damming of the Colorado River. The park was created to give public access to the lake's calm waters and to protect the surrounding granite outcrops, wildflower meadows, and oak-juniper forest.

The area was once home to Tonkawa and Comanche tribes, and later became popular with ranchers and vacationers. Inks Lake is unique because its water level stays relatively constant year-round, making it one of the most swim-friendly and boat-friendly lakes in the Texas Hill Country.

Top Trails & Sites Visited

- ☐ Devil's Waterhole Trail (0.2 mi)
- ☐ Valley Spring Creek Trail (0.9 mi)
- ☐ Devil's Backbone Nat Trail (1.3 mi)
- ☐ Lake Trail (1.2 mi)
- ☐ Pecan Flats Trail (1.8 mi)
- ☐ Other: _______________________

Date of Visit: _______________________

Where did you stay? _______________________

Who were you with? _______________________

What did you do? _______________________

Favorite Memories? _______________________

Interesting Facts

- Inks Lake has a popular swimming hole called "Devil's Waterhole", surrounded by pink granite cliffs.
- The park sits on ancient Precambrian granite, more than a billion years old.
- Wildflowers, including bluebonnets and Indian paintbrush, bloom here each spring.
- The park rents out kayaks, canoes, and paddle boats from a lakeside boathouse.
- It's a dark-sky friendly area — great for stargazing on clear nights.

State Park Stamp

Park Website

Park Maps

Lake Brownwood State Park

200 State Highway Park Road 15, Lake Brownwood, TX 76801 – Hours: Open daily from 6 AM to 10 PM

2X3 photo

History

Lake Brownwood State Park was constructed by the Civilian Conservation Corps (CCC) in the 1930s and **officially opened in 1938**. CCC Company 849 built the park's infrastructure, including stone bridges, picnic structures, and the impressive Lone Star Lodge, which still stands today.

The lake itself was created by damming Pecan Bayou, a tributary of the Colorado River, following severe floods in the 1920s. Once completed, the reservoir offered a source of recreation, water, and flood control for the area — and the park became one of the early CCC showpieces of the Texas State Parks system.

Top Trails & Sites Visited

☐ Council Bluff Nature Trail (0.3 mi)
☐ Lakeside Trail (0.7 mi)
☐ Texas Oak Trail (1.4 mi)
☐ Opossum Loop (1.1 mi)
☐ CCC Grand Stairway
☐ Other: _______________________

Date of Visit: _______________________________________

Where did you stay? _______________________________________

Who were you with? _______________________________________

What did you do? _______________________________________

Favorite Memories? _______________________________________

____

State Park Stamp

Interesting Facts

- The Lone Star Lodge and dining hall are available for overnight group rental.
- The park features a historic stone observation tower overlooking the lake.
- Several CCC-built buildings and picnic tables are still in use today.
- Known for incredible fall sunsets over the lake's western shore.
- The lake is popular for white bass and catfish fishing, especially in spring.

Park Website

Park Maps

Visit the Texas Parks & Wildlife Department at tpwd.texas.gov

Lake Somerville State Park

Nails Creek: 6280 FM 180, Ledbetter, TX 78946 - Birch Creek: 14222 Park Road 57, Somerville, TX 77879
Hours: Open daily from 6 AM to 10 PM

2X3 photo

History

Lake Somerville State Park **opened in 1970** and was created to support recreation on Lake Somerville, a U.S. Army Corps of Engineers reservoir completed in the 1960s. The park is divided into two main units — Birch Creek (north side of the lake) and Nails Creek (south side) — connected by the Somerville Trailway, a 13-mile multiuse path that winds through forest, prairie, and wetland.

The area was historically occupied by Tonkawa Tribe and other native peoples and later supported cattle ranching and agriculture. Today, it's known for boating, hiking, horseback riding, and birdwatching.

Top Trails & Sites Visited

☐ Honeybee Hill Trail (0.4 mi)
☐ Wilderness Run (1.3 mi)
☐ Sunset Trail (0.9 mi)
☐ Flag Pond Loop (1.7 mi)
☐ Eagle Point
☐ Other:_____________________

Date of Visit: ____

Where did you stay? ____

Who were you with? ____

What did you do? ____

Favorite Memories? ____

____

Interesting Facts

- The 13-mile Lake Somerville Trailway connects Birch Creek and Nails Creek Units — and is open to hikers, bikers, and equestrians.
- The lake is well-stocked with white bass, crappie, and catfish, and has multiple boat ramps and fishing piers.
- During rainy years, the park features wetland habitats that attract hundreds of migratory birds.
- Equestrian camping is available at Nails Creek, with horse pens and trail access.

State Park Stamp

Park Website

Park Maps

Lake Whitney State Park

433 FM 1244, Whitney, TX 76692   –   Hours: Open daily from 6 AM to 10 PM

2X3 photo

History

Lake Whitney State Park **opened in 1965**, shortly after the construction of Lake Whitney, a large reservoir created in 1951 by damming the Brazos River. The park was developed to provide access to the lake's rocky bluffs, coves, and rolling hills, which had been used for ranching and hunting since the 1800s.

In addition to recreation, the park serves as a protected zone for several rare plant species and migratory bird habitats. Its scenic views and deep lake have made it a go-to weekend escape for North Texans.

Top Trails & Sites Visited

☐ Towash Forest Trail (1.2 mi)
☐ Two Bridges Trail (0.9 mi)
☐ Lake View Point
☐ Towash Settlement
☐ Other: _______________________
☐ Other: _______________________

Date of Visit: ____

Where did you stay? ____

Who were you with? ____

What did you do? ____

Favorite Memories? ____

____

____

State Park Stamp

Interesting Facts

- Offers multiple shaded campsites with lake views and water access.
- Known for catfish, crappie, and striped bass fishing — both onshore and by boat.
- Home to seasonal wildflower blooms, including bluebonnets and prairie verbena.
- Rangers host night sky programs and wildlife hikes during peak seasons.
- The park's limestone bluffs are great for sunset views and photography.

Park Website

Park Maps

Visit the Texas Parks & Wildlife Department at tpwd.texas.gov

Lockhart State Park

2012 State Park Road, Lockhart, TX 78644 - Hours: Open daily from 8 AM to 10 PM

2X3 photo

History

Lockhart State Park was **built in the 1930s** by the Civilian Conservation Corps (CCC) on land donated by local citizens. Originally intended for both recreation and water conservation, the park includes stonework, trails, and pavilions built by CCC workers.

What makes Lockhart especially unique is its 9-hole public golf course, one of only a few located inside a state park. In addition to golfing, visitors enjoy trails, a creek for fishing, and easy access to the famed BBQ capital of Texas — the town of Lockhart itself.

Top Trails & Sites Visited

- ☐ Clear Fork Trail (0.4 mi)
- ☐ Creekview Trail (0.3 mi)
- ☐ Wild Rose Loop (0.4 mi)
- ☐ Hill Top Trail (0.3 mi)
- ☐ Historic Golf Course
- ☐ Other: _______________________

Date of Visit: _______________________

Where did you stay? _______________________

Who were you with? _______________________

What did you do? _______________________

Favorite Memories? _______________________

Interesting Facts

- The 9-hole golf course is open to the public year-round, with gear rentals and carts available.
- Trails wind through oak-wooded hills, a historic CCC dam, and Clear Fork Creek.
- The CCC stonework throughout the park includes a recreation hall, pavilion, and rock bridges.
- The park features a seasonal swimming pool (closed for renovation in some seasons — check website).
- You can fish for sunfish, catfish, and bass — no license required from the shore.

State Park Stamp

Park Website

Park Maps

Longhorn Cavern State Park

6211 Park Road 4 South, Burnet, TX 78611 - Hours: Open daily from 8 AM to 4:30 PM

2X3 photo

History

Longhorn Cavern became a state park in 1932 and **officially opened in 1937** after extensive development by the Civilian Conservation Corps (CCC). The CCC built the administration building, stone walkways, and park infrastructure — while also clearing hundreds of tons of debris from the cavern itself. The cavern has a rich and mysterious history: once used by Native Americans, it later served as a Confederate saltpeter mine, a hideout for outlaws, and even a dance hall and speakeasy in the 1920s. Its unique limestone formations and underground chambers make it one of Texas's most geologically significant and culturally intriguing parks.

Please note: Day use park only - no camping
Cave tours require tickets

Top Trails & Sites Visited

☐ Blakbone Ridge Nat. Trail (0.35 mi)
☐ Karst Discovery Trail (0.60 mi)
☐ Wildflower Way (0.10 mi)
☐ Wild Cave Tour
☐ Stone Lookout Tower
☐ Other: _______________________

Date of Visit: ____

Where did you stay? ____

Who were you with? ____

What did you do? ____

Favorite Memories? ____

____

____

State Park Stamp

Interesting Facts

- Longhorn Cavern is a "river-formed" cave, not a traditional dripstone cavern — formed by ancient underground streams.
- One of the cave's large rooms once hosted underground ballroom dances and concerts.
- Legend claims the outlaw Sam Bass hid treasure inside the cave.
- The park's observation tower offers panoramic Hill Country views.
- Day use park only - no camping; Cave tours require tickets.

Park Website   Park Maps

Visit the Texas Parks & Wildlife Department at tpwd.texas.gov

Lost Maples State Natural Area

2038 Lost Maples Park Road, Vanderpool, TX 78885 - Hours: Open daily from 8 AM to 8 PM

2X3 photo

History

Lost Maples State Natural Area was **established in 1979** to protect one of the last stands of Uvalde bigtooth maples in Texas. The park is renowned for its spectacular fall foliage, attracting visitors from across the state.

The area was historically used by Native American tribes and later by settlers for ranching. Preservation efforts have kept the park's unique ecosystem intact, with its rugged canyons and clear streams serving as a haven for diverse wildlife.

Top Trails & Sites Visited

☐ Maple Trail (0.4 mi)
☐ East-West Trail (1 mi)
☐ West Loop Trail (2.9 mi)
☐ Monkey Rock
☐ Grotto
☐ Other: _______________________

Date of Visit: ____

Where did you stay? ____

Who were you with? ____

What did you do? ____

Favorite Memories? ____

____

____

Interesting Facts

- Lost Maples features a rare Texas native maple tree species that creates vibrant colors in autumn, a rarity in this part of the state.
- The park's rugged terrain includes several limestone canyons carved by seasonal streams.
- It's designated as a Natural Area by TPWD, meaning it's protected for research and conservation.
- Nighttime offers excellent stargazing opportunities due to minimal light pollution.

State Park Stamp

Park Website

Park Maps

Visit the Texas Parks & Wildlife Department at tpwd.texas.gov

Lyndon B. Johnson State Park

199 Park Road 52, Stonewall, TX 78671 - Hours: Open daily from 8 AM to 4:30 PM

2X3 photo

History

This park honors President Lyndon B. Johnson, the 36th President of the United States and native of the Texas Hill Country. **Established in 1970**, it lies directly across the Pedernales River from the LBJ Ranch (part of the Lyndon B. Johnson National Historical Park) and was built on land donated by the Johnson family.

In addition to offering traditional state park recreation, this site includes the Sauer-Beckmann Living History Farm, which authentically recreates farm life in 1918. The park blends presidential history with German-Texan heritage, scenic trails, and wildlife viewing in the heart of Hill Country

Top Trails & Sites Visited

☐ Sauer-Beckmann Living His. Farm
☐ Aquatic Complex
☐ Other: _______________________
☐ Other: _______________________
☐ Other: _______________________
☐ Other: _______________________

Date of Visit: ____

Where did you stay? ____

Who were you with? ____

What did you do? ____

Favorite Memories? ____

____

____

Interesting Facts

- President Johnson's boyhood home and Texas White House are visible just across the river from the park.
- The Sauer-Beckmann Farm staff dress in period clothing and perform daily chores using 1918-era tools and techniques.
- A portion of the park is managed as bison and longhorn pasture — both species were important to LBJ's conservation work.
- It's one of the only Texas state parks with free admission year-round.

State Park Stamp

Park Website

Park Maps

Visit the Texas Parks & Wildlife Department at tpwd.texas.gov

McKinney Falls State Park

5808 McKinney Falls Parkway, Austin, TX 78744 - Hours: Open daily from 8 AM to 10 PM

2X3 photo

History

McKinney Falls State Park **opened in 1976** and is named after Thomas F. McKinney, a prominent early settler, businessman, and one of Stephen F. Austin's "Old Three Hundred." He established a homestead and gristmill here in the 1850s. Ruins of his stone house and mill remain as part of the park's cultural history.

Nestled within the city of Austin, the park protects over 700 acres of woodland, limestone cliffs, and Onion Creek — which flows dramatically over Upper and Lower McKinney Falls. Despite its urban setting, the park offers a surprisingly wild escape with miles of hiking trails, historic sites, and swimming holes.

Top Trails & Sites Visited

- ☐ Homestead Trail (3.1 mi)
- ☐ Onion Creek Trail (2.8 mi)
- ☐ Rock Shelter Trail (0.6 mi)
- ☐ Picnic Trail + Lower Falls (0.5 mi)
- ☐ Upper Falls
- ☐ Other: _______________________

Date of Visit: ____

Where did you stay? ____

Who were you with? ____

What did you do? ____

Favorite Memories? ____

____

____

Interesting Facts

- You can swim directly beneath two natural limestone waterfalls: Upper and Lower Falls.
- The El Camino Real de los Tejas National Historic Trail passes through the park.
- Onion Creek can flash flood quickly, creating dramatic water surges after heavy rain.
- The Smith Rock Shelter in the park was used by native peoples over 4,000 years ago.
- Popular with locals for trail running, dog walking, and mountain biking — just 15 minutes from downtown Austin.

State Park Stamp

Park Website

Park Maps

Meridian State Park

173 Park Road 7, Meridian, TX 76665   -   Hours: Open daily from 6 AM to 10 PM

2X3 photo

History

Meridian State Park **opened in 1935** as part of Texas' early conservation efforts and was built by the Civilian Conservation Corps (CCC). CCC Company constructed park roads, trails, shelters, and a dam that formed Lake Meridian, a spring-fed 72-acre reservoir at the heart of the park.

The area was once part of a ranching community and is now home to protected native prairie, oak-juniper woodlands, and scenic limestone bluffs. Its small size, peaceful setting, and unique wildlife make it a favorite weekend retreat for nature lovers in the Waco region.

Top Trails & Sites Visited

- ☐ Little Forest Junior Trail (0.8 mi)
- ☐ Shinnery Ridge Trail (1.5 mi)
- ☐ Little Springs Trail (0.7 mi)
- ☐ Bosque Hiking Trail (2.2 mi)
- ☐ Bee Ledge
- ☐ Other: ______________________

Date of Visit: ____

Where did you stay? ____

Who were you with? ____

What did you do? ____

Favorite Memories? ____

____

____

State Park Stamp

Interesting Facts

- The Bosque Hiking Trail wraps around the entire lake and crosses over the CCC dam.
- The park is a habitat for the endangered golden-cheeked warbler, seen in spring.
- You can rent kayaks and paddle boats to explore the calm lake waters.
- CCC-built stone shelters and fireplaces are still in use around the lake.
- It's a designated "Lone Star Legacy Park", honoring its historic and cultural significance.

Park Website

Park Maps

Visit the Texas Parks & Wildlife Department at tpwd.texas.gov

Mother Neff State Park

1680 TX-236, Moody, TX 76557 - Hours: Open daily from 8 AM to 10 PM

2X3 photo

History

Established in 1921, Mother Neff State Park is recognized as the **first official state park in Texas**. It was named in honor of Isadora "Mother" Neff, mother of Texas Governor Pat Neff, who donated the initial 6 acres of land that would grow into the park.

The Civilian Conservation Corps (CCC) helped shape the park in the 1930s, building stone shelters, trails, and its iconic rock tower overlook. The park's natural beauty includes limestone outcrops, cedar and oak forest, and a stretch of the Leon River. Despite occasional flooding, the park remains a quiet refuge with historical depth and scenic charm.

Top Trails & Sites Visited

- ☐ Wash Pond Trail (0.5 mi)
- ☐ Tower Trail (0.6 mi)
- ☐ Prairie Loop (0.6 mi)
- ☐ CCC Rock Tower
- ☐ Tonkawa Cave
- ☐ Other: ___________________

Date of Visit: ____

Where did you stay? ____

Who were you with? ____

What did you do? ____

Favorite Memories? ____

____

____

Interesting Facts

- The CCC stone water tower is still standing and offers views of the surrounding countryside.
- The park was dedicated in 1937 as a tribute to public service and conservation.
- Several park features are made of local limestone, hand-chiseled by CCC workers.
- Interpretive signs share stories about early Texas park history and the Neff family.
- The park offers free Junior Ranger activity packs for kids to explore the site.

State Park Stamp

Park Website

Park Maps

Palmetto State Park

78 Park Road 11 South, Gonzales, TX 78629 - Hours: Open daily from 8 AM to 10 PM

2X3 photo

History

Palmetto State Park **opened in 1936** and was one of Texas's early CCC-era parks. It's named for the dwarf palmetto palms that grow naturally along the swampy banks of Ottine Swamp, a rare ecosystem in Central Texas.

The park was developed to preserve the tropical-like habitat and spring-fed areas of the San Marcos River, which flows along its border. CCC stonework, a scenic oxbow lake, and warm spring-fed wetlands make this park a surprising and peaceful escape.

Top Trails & Sites Visited

☐ Mossycup Spur (0.3 mi)
☐ Oxbow Lake Trail (0.7 mi)
☐ San Marcos Trail (1.3 mi)
☐ Extinct Mud Boils
☐ Artrsian Well
☐ Other: ________________________

Date of Visit: ____

Where did you stay? ____

Who were you with? ____

What did you do? ____

Favorite Memories? ____

____

State Park Stamp

Interesting Facts

- Dwarf palmettos usually grow along the Gulf Coast — their presence here is rare inland.
- The park includes a CCC-era refectory and water tower, still in use today.
- A spring-fed oxbow lake is open for paddling and fishing year-round.
- The area has long been home to legends of ghost sightings and swamp creatures — making it a local favorite for spooky stories.
- The Ottine Swamp supports dozens of bird species and unusual wetland plants.

Park Website   Park Maps

Visit the Texas Parks & Wildlife Department at tpwd.texas.gov

Pedernales Falls State Park

2585 Park Road 6026, Johnson City, TX 78636 – Hours: Open daily from 8 AM to 10 PM

2X3 photo

History

Established in 1971, Pedernales Falls State Park spans over 5,200 acres along the Pedernales River, a tributary of the Colorado River. Known for its dramatic limestone cascades and sculpted riverbeds, the park was once part of the Circle Bar Ranch before the state purchased it for conservation and recreation.

The river's name comes from the Spanish word "pedernal" meaning "flint" — due to the abundance of flint rock along the riverbed. The park has become one of Texas' top destinations for hiking, photography, swimming, and stargazing in the Hill Country.

Top Trails & Sites Visited

- ☐ Falls Overlook Trail (0.3 mi)
- ☐ Hackenburg Trail (1.4 mi)
- ☐ Pedernales Falls Trail (1.8 mi)
- ☐ Wolf Mountain Trail (7.0 mi)
- ☐ Pedernales Falls
- ☐ Other: _______________________

Date of Visit: _______________________________________

Where did you stay? _________________________________

Who were you with? _________________________________

What did you do? ____________________________________

Favorite Memories? __________________________________

____

Interesting Facts

- The main falls area is made of massive slabs of ancient limestone, shaped by erosion over thousands of years.
- The river can rise several feet in minutes during flash floods — warning sirens are installed for safety.
- The park's scenic overlook is popular for sunset photography and birdwatching.
- There are over 20 miles of hiking and mountain biking trails, including remote backcountry loops.
- The Twin Falls Nature Trail leads to a hidden double waterfall tucked in a rocky grotto.

State Park Stamp

Park Website

Park Maps

South Llano River State Park

1927 Park Road 73, Junction, TX 76849 - Hours: Open daily from 8 AM to 10 PM

2X3 photo

History

South Llano River State Park **opened in 1990** on land donated by Walter Buck Jr., a conservationist and local rancher who wanted to preserve the land's natural beauty. The park spans more than 2,600 acres of Hill Country wilderness, with the clear-flowing South Llano River running along its northern boundary.

Before state ownership, this land was part of a working ranch and wildlife refuge. Today, it supports outdoor activities and protects critical habitat for the Rio Grande turkey, which roost in the park's trees each fall and winter.

Top Trails & Sites Visited

- ☐ Buck Lake Trail (1.6 mi)
- ☐ Fawn Trail (1.3 mi)
- ☐ Overlook Trail (0.9 mi)
- ☐ Frisbee Trail (2.3 mi)
- ☐ Old Barn
- ☐ Other: _______________________

Date of Visit: _______________________________________

Where did you stay? _______________________________________

Who were you with? _______________________________________

What did you do? _______________________________________

Favorite Memories? _______________________________________

____

____

State Park Stamp

Interesting Facts

- The park is a designated International Dark Sky Park, perfect for stargazing.
- Over 20 miles of trails for hikers and bikers weave through wooded hills and rocky ridges.
- In winter, large sections are closed to protect roosting Rio Grande turkeys.
- The park is part of the Texas Hill Country Wildlife Trail, making it a birding hotspot.
- Visitors love to float, kayak, or wade the spring-fed river during warmer months.

Park Website   Park Maps

Visit the Texas Parks & Wildlife Department at tpwd.texas.gov

Abilene State Park

150 Park Road 32, Tuscola, TX 79562 – Hours: Open daily from 8 AM to 10 PM

<table><tr><td>

2X3 photo

</td><td>

History

Established in 1934, Abilene State Park was developed by the Civilian Conservation Corps (CCC) and remains one of Texas's classic early state parks. It lies at the foot of Elm Creek Reservoir (formerly Lake Abilene) and features stonework architecture, pecan groves, and grassy campgrounds designed for family recreation.

Originally part of a private ranch, the land was gifted to the state for public enjoyment. Though the reservoir has experienced water level issues, the park remains a favorite for reunions, scout groups, and nature getaways.

Top Trails & Sites Visited
☐ Eagle Trail (0.2 mi)
☐ Elm Creek Nature Trail (0.9 mi)
☐ Legacy Trail (0.2 mi)
☐ Roadrunner Trail (1.5 mi)
☐ Buffalo Wallow
☐ Other: _______________________

</td></tr></table>

Date of Visit: ____

Where did you stay? ____

Who were you with? ____

What did you do? ____

Favorite Memories? ____

____

____

Interesting Facts

- The CCC built the stone water tower, swimming pool, and picnic pavilion, all still in use.
- The park is known for its massive, shady pecan trees lining trails and campsites.
- Visitors can stay in rustic screened shelters or a glamping-style yurt.
- It's just minutes from the historic town of Buffalo Gap, home to a frontier museum and famous steakhouse.
- Birdwatchers and butterfly lovers flock here for seasonal migrations.

State Park Stamp

Park Website

Park Maps

Balmorhea State Park

9207 TX-17, Toyahvale, TX 79786   -   Hours: Open daily from 8 AM to 7:30 PM

2X3 photo

History

Balmorhea State Park was developed by the Civilian Conservation Corps (CCC) during the Great Depression and **opened in 1936**. The CCC engineers tapped into San Solomon Springs, which naturally discharges more than 15 million gallons of water per day, to build the park's massive, spring fed swimming pool — still one of the largest in the world.

The springs have been an oasis for centuries, first used by Native American tribes like the Mescalero Apache, then later by Mexican settlers and frontier ranchers. The pool and surrounding wetlands now form a critical habitat for endangered species and a beloved recreational site in the arid West Texas desert.

Top Trails & Sites Visited

☐ Spring-Fed Pool Area
☐ Cienega Observation Deck
☐ San Solomon Springs Overlook
☐ Other: _______________________
☐ Other: _______________________
☐ Other: _______________________

Date of Visit: ____

Where did you stay? ____

Who were you with? ____

What did you do? ____

Favorite Memories? ____

____

State Park Stamp

Interesting Facts

- Balmorhea's pool holds 3.5 million gallons of water and reaches depths of 25 feet.
- It is home to two endangered desert fish: the Comanche Springs pupfish and Pecos gambusia.
- The pool stays a consistent 72–76°F year-round, making it ideal for winter swims.
- Scuba diving is permitted with a dive permit — one of the few Texas parks that allows it.
- The CCC also constructed adobe-style buildings, including the historic San Solomon Courts motel (still in use).

Park Website

Park Maps

Visit the Texas Parks & Wildlife Department at tpwd.texas.gov

Barton Warnock Visitor Center

FM 170, Lajitas, TX 79852 - Hours: Open daily from 8 AM to 4:30 PM

2X3 photo

History

The Barton Warnock Visitor Center, **opened in 1991**, serves as the eastern gateway to Big Bend Ranch State Park — the largest and wildest of all Texas state parks. Named after Dr. Barton H. Warnock, a noted botanist and desert scholar, the center features a museum-quality exhibit hall that introduces visitors to the natural and cultural history of the Chihuahuan Desert.

The land surrounding the center is part of the rugged Rio Grande corridor and includes scenic desert hills, cactus gardens, and access to one of Texas's most beautiful scenic drives — FM 170, the River Road.

Top Trails & Sites Visited

☐ Other: _______________________
☐ Other: _______________________
☐ Other: _______________________
☐ Other: _______________________

*this visitor center is located at big bend ranch, and does not have its own trails.

Date of Visit: ____

Where did you stay? ____

Who were you with? ____

What did you do? ____

Favorite Memories? ____

____

Interesting Facts

- The site includes the "Una Tierra – One Land" museum exhibit, which interprets millions of years of geology, plant life, and human history in the region.
- This is the primary entrance station for Big Bend Ranch State Park, which spans over 300,000 acres.
- The center offers permits for backcountry use, maps, and local advice from rangers.
- FM 170 nearby is nicknamed the "most scenic drive in Texas," offering jaw-dropping views of the Rio Grande.

State Park Stamp

Park Website

Park Maps

Visit the Texas Parks & Wildlife Department at tpwd.texas.gov

Big Bend Ranch State Park

1900 Sauceda Ranch Rd, Presidio, TX 79845   -   Hours: Open daily from 8 AM to 6 PM

2X3 photo

History

Big Bend Ranch State Park was **officially designated in 1988**, but the area has a long and rugged history. Once home to Native American tribes, including the Jumano, Apache, and Comanche, it later became a corridor for explorers, miners, and ranchers. The land was privately ranched for over a century before being acquired by the state.

At over 311,000 acres, it is the largest state park in Texas, encompassing desert mountains, volcanic formations, Rio Grande riverfront, and remote canyons. Known for its raw beauty and isolation, Big Bend Ranch complements its national park neighbor — but is far less crowded and more ruggedly wild.

Top Trails & Sites Visited

- ☐ Contrabandista Spur (0.6 mi)
- ☐ Crystal Trail (1.3 mi)
- ☐ Rock Quarry Trail (1.0 mi)
- ☐ Other: _______________________
- ☐ Other: _______________________
- ☐ Other: _______________________

Date of Visit: _______________________________________

Where did you stay? ___________________________________

Who were you with? ___________________________________

What did you do? _____________________________________

Favorite Memories? ___________________________________

____

____

State Park Stamp

Interesting Facts

- The park is a Dark Sky Park, making it one of the best places for stargazing in Texas.
- Its most famous trail, Closed Canyon, winds through a narrow slot canyon formed by erosion.
- The park contains volcanic tuff, lava flows, and hoodoos, giving it otherworldly terrain.
- You can drive the 100-mile "River Road" (FM 170) along the Rio Grande for epic views.
- Several abandoned ranching sites and mining relics can be explored via remote trails.

Park Website

Park Maps

Visit the Texas Parks & Wildlife Department at tpwd.texas.gov

Big Spring State Park

1 Scenic Dr, Big Spring, TX 79720 - Hours: Open daily from 8 AM to Sunset

2X3 photo

History

Big Spring State Park **opened in 1936** and was built largely by the Works Progress Administration (WPA) and Civilian Conservation Corps (CCC) during the Great Depression. The park sits atop a 200-foot bluff offering panoramic views of the surrounding plains.

The area was historically significant as a natural spring and meeting place for Native Americans, early settlers, and military expeditions. Although the spring itself is no longer flowing, the park preserves the history and natural beauty of this West Texas landmark.

Top Trails & Sites Visited

☐ Scenic Mountain Loop (4.0 mi)
☐ Outer Limits Trail (1.2 mi)
☐ Nature Trail (0.4 mi)
☐ Sotol Stroll Loop (0.6 mi)
☐ Other: _______________________
☐ Other: _______________________

Date of Visit: ____

Where did you stay? ____

Who were you with? ____

What did you do? ____

Favorite Memories? ____

____

____

Interesting Facts

- A 3-mile scenic drive circles the park's bluff, popular with runners and cyclists.
- The park pavilion and stone walls were crafted from locally quarried limestone by WPA crews.
- From the bluff, you can view miles of rolling plains and oil country.
- The "Big Spring" that gave the city its name once bubbled near the base of the bluff.
- Despite its small size, the park hosts local festivals, picnics, and stargazing events.

State Park Stamp

Park Website

Park Maps

Visit the Texas Parks & Wildlife Department at tpwd.texas.gov

Davis Mountains State Park

TX-118 N, Fort Davis, TX 79734   -   Hours: Open daily from 8 AM to 10 PM

2X3 photo

History

Davis Mountains State Park was one of the original parks developed by the Civilian Conservation Corps (CCC) in the 1930s and **opened in 1938**. CCC Company built roads, trails, picnic shelters, and the park's crown jewel: Indian Lodge, a pueblo-style adobe hotel nestled in the mountains.

The land sits near historic Fort Davis, a key frontier military post. The region has long been home to Apache peoples and later settlers, ranchers, and travelers through the mountain pass. Today, the park is cherished for its high elevation, cool temperatures, scenic drives, and panoramic hiking trails.

Top Trails & Sites Visited

☐ Skyline Drive Trail (2.6 mi)
☐ Montézuma Quail Trail (0.9 mi)
☐ Indian Lodge Trail (1.5 mi)
☐ Indian Lodge
☐ Headquarters Trail (0.3 mi)
☐ Other: _______________________

Date of Visit: ____

Where did you stay? ____

Who were you with? ____

What did you do? ____

Favorite Memories? ____

____

State Park Stamp

Interesting Facts

- The park sits at over 5,000 feet elevation, making it cooler and greener than most of West Texas.
- Indian Lodge, a 1930s adobe hotel, still operates as a full-service lodge with 39 rooms.
- The park offers access to Fort Davis National Historic Site via a scenic trail.
- Birdwatchers come from all over to spot Montezuma quail, hummingbirds, and more.
- The Skyline Drive offers sweeping views and stone overlook shelters built by the CCC.

Park Website

Park Maps

Visit the Texas Parks & Wildlife Department at tpwd.texas.gov

Devils River State Natural Area

21715 Dolan Creek Rd, Del Rio, TX 78840 - Hours: Open daily from 8 AM to 5 PM; Reservation ONLY

2X3 photo

History

Devils River State Natural Area protects a remote stretch of the Devils River, one of the cleanest, clearest rivers in Texas. Originally a ranch, the 37,000+ acre site was purchased by Texas Parks and Wildlife in the **1980s** and later expanded with conservation grants. The river and its canyons have been visited for thousands of years, with Indigenous rock art sites and historic ranching remains scattered throughout the landscape.

This is not a typical state park — it's a backcountry wilderness experience, intended for well-prepared visitors with high-clearance vehicles and outdoor experience.

Top Trails & Sites Visited

☐ Other: _______________________
☐ Other: _______________________
☐ Other: _______________________
☐ Other: _______________________

*this visitor center is located at big bend ranch, and does not have its own trails.

Date of Visit: ____

Where did you stay? _______________________________________

Who were you with? _______________________________________

What did you do? ____

Favorite Memories? _______________________________________

____

Interesting Facts

- The Devils River is spring-fed, giving it turquoise clarity and strong year-round flow.
- The site contains prehistoric rock art panels from ancient Indigenous cultures.
- It's one of the few parks in Texas where paddling permits and overnight river use are tightly regulated.
- Access requires navigating a 22-mile gravel road, often impassable in rain.
- The park has dark sky conditions ideal for stargazing and astrophotography.

State Park Stamp

Park Website

Park Maps

Visit the Texas Parks & Wildlife Department at tpwd.texas.gov

Devil's Sinkhole State Natural Area

101 N. Sweeten St., Rocksprings, TX 78880 – Hours: Guided Tour ONLY, Reservations REQUIRED

2X3 photo

History

Devil's Sinkhole was designated a **National Natural Landmark in 1985** and became part of the Texas State Parks system in 1995. The site features a massive limestone cavern with a vertical shaft over 140 feet deep and a main cavern room measuring over 320 feet wide.

The area was long known to Native Americans, early explorers, and local ranchers. Today, it's protected not only for its geology, but also as a seasonal roosting site for up to 3 million Mexican free-tailed bats, making it one of the largest bat colonies in Texas.

Top Trails & Sites Visited

☐ Other: _______________________
☐ Other: _______________________
☐ Other: _______________________
☐ Other: _______________________

Guided Tour ONLY. No maps available to view online.

Date of Visit: _______________________

Where did you stay? _______________________

Who were you with? _______________________

What did you do? _______________________

Favorite Memories? _______________________

____

____

State Park Stamp

Interesting Facts

- The sinkhole drops more than 140 feet straight down and is over 350 feet deep in total.
- It's home to millions of bats that emerge dramatically at dusk between May and October.
- The only way to access the site is via guided tours, preserving its sensitive ecosystem.
- A permanent bat-viewing platform allows for safe, ranger-led observation of evening flights.
- The cavern has been explored by cave divers and contains rare geologic formations.

Park Website   Park Maps

Visit the Texas Parks & Wildlife Department at tpwd.texas.gov

Fort Leaton State Historic Site

16952 FM 170, Presidio, TX 79845 - Hours: Open daily from 8 AM to 4:30 PM

2X3 photo

History

Fort Leaton was **established in 1848** by Benjamin Leaton, who converted an old Spanish hacienda into a frontier trading post and fortified home. It played a key role in trade between Texas and Mexico, supplying travelers, settlers, and military convoys moving along the Chihuahua Trail.

The fort was abandoned after Leaton's death and slowly fell into ruin before being restored in the 20th century. Now managed by TPWD, Fort Leaton serves as the western entrance station to Big Bend Ranch State Park and a rare example of borderland adobe fortress architecture.

Top Trails & Sites Visited

☐ Other: _______________________

☐ Other: _______________________

☐ Other: _______________________

☐ Other: _______________________

*this visitor center is located at big bend ranch, and does not have its own trails.

Date of Visit: _______________________

Where did you stay? _______________________

Who were you with? _______________________

What did you do? _______________________

Favorite Memories? _______________________

Interesting Facts

- The original structure contains 2-foot thick adobe walls, providing insulation and defense.
- The fort housed everything from a blacksmith shop and granary to family quarters and defensive towers.
- It once served as a diplomatic and trade hub between Texas and northern Mexico.
- Visitors can still see bullet holes in the adobe from past frontier conflicts.
- Fort Leaton is a prime example of Spanish-Mexican vernacular architecture in Texas.

State Park Stamp

Park Website

Park Maps

Franklin Mountains State Park

2900 Tom Mays Access Rd, El Paso, TX 79911   -   Hours: Open daily from 8 AM to 5 PM

2X3 photo

History

Established in 1987, Franklin Mountains State Park protects nearly 27,000 acres of Chihuahuan Desert landscape — making it one of the largest urban wilderness parks in the country. The rugged Franklin range, made of ancient volcanic rock and uplifted fault-block formations, dominates the skyline of El Paso.

The area has been used for thousands of years, from early Native American peoples to Spanish colonists and Mexican revolutionaries. Today, the park offers miles of remote-feeling hiking and biking trails, despite being just minutes from downtown El Paso.

Top Trails & Sites Visited

- ☐ Aztec Caves Trail (1.9 mi)
- ☐ Nature Walk Trail (0.75 mi)
- ☐ Upper Sunset Trail (1.3 mi)
- ☐ Lower Sunset (3.6 mi)
- ☐ Schaffer Shuffle(2.6 mi)
- ☐ Other: _______________________

Date of Visit: ____

Where did you stay? ____

Who were you with? ____

What did you do? ____

Favorite Memories? ____

____

____

State Park Stamp

Interesting Facts

- The Franklins are over 1 billion years old, among the oldest mountains in Texas.
- The park contains El Paso's highest peak — North Franklin Mountain (7,192 ft).
- It has over 100 miles of trails for hiking, mountain biking, and trail running.
- Rattlesnake Ridge and Mundy's Gap are popular for panoramic views.
- Bats emerge seasonally from caves near the Aztec Caves Trail at dusk.

Park Website   Park Maps

Visit the Texas Parks & Wildlife Department at tpwd.texas.gov

Government Canyon State Natural Area

12861 Galm Rd, San Antonio, TX 78254 - Hours: Open F - M from 7 AM to 10 PM; Closed T-Th

2X3 photo

History

Government Canyon State Natural Area protects over 12,000 acres of rugged Hill Country terrain, established to conserve the Edwards Aquifer recharge zone — San Antonio's primary water source. The area **opened to the public in 2005** after decades of conservation efforts.

The land features a mix of canyons, limestone ridges, and savannah — and is most famous for housing over 110-million-year-old dinosaur tracks, preserved in the bedrock of a seasonal creek. In addition to offering miles of trails, the site also focuses on education, aquifer protection, and ecological restoration.

Top Trails & Sites Visited

- ☐ Savannah Loop (2.6 mi)
- ☐ Lytle's Loop (0.7 mi)
- ☐ North Bluff Spurs Overlook(3.4 mi)
- ☐ Joe Johnston Route (0.3 mi)
- ☐ Zizelmann House
- ☐ Other: _______________________

Date of Visit: _______________________________________

Where did you stay? _______________________________

Who were you with? _______________________________

What did you do? _________________________________

Favorite Memories? _______________________________

____

____

Interesting Facts

- Dinosaur tracks from Acrocanthosaurus and Sauroposeidon are preserved in the park's limestone beds.
- More than 40 miles of trails are divided into "Frontcountry" (easier) and "Backcountry" (more rugged) loops.
- The park protects oak-juniper savannas, endangered species, and aquifer recharge lands.
- Government Canyon is a no-dog zone on trails — to protect sensitive wildlife and ecosystems.

State Park Stamp

Park Website

Park Maps

Visit the Texas Parks & Wildlife Department at tpwd.texas.gov

Hill Country State Natural Area

10600 Bandera Creek Rd, Bandera, TX 78003 - Hours: Open daily from 8 AM to 5 PM

2X3 photo

History

Hill Country State Natural Area was once part of the Bar-O Ranch, a historic working cattle ranch, and was **gifted to the state in 1976**. The land covers over 5,300 acres of undeveloped Texas Hill Country, and it remains one of the most primitive and wild parks in the system.

Designed to offer minimal development, the park emphasizes solitude, backcountry hiking, and equestrian use. It's known for its limestone hills, dry creek beds, scenic ridges, and vast views. The park remains a favorite for those seeking quiet trails, horseback riding, or a real wilderness escape.

Top Trails & Sites Visited

☐ Merrick Mile Trail (1 mi)
☐ Heritage Loop (1.1 mi)
☐ Wilderness Trail (3.1 mi)
☐ Hermits Trail (0.3 mi)
☐ Comanche Bluff
☐ Other: _______________________

Date of Visit: ____

Where did you stay? ____

Who were you with? ____

What did you do? ____

Favorite Memories? ____

____

____

State Park Stamp

Interesting Facts

- Over 40 miles of multi-use trails make this one of Texas's top equestrian destinations.
- The park has no RV hookups or modern restrooms, preserving its primitive nature.
- Originally part of the Bar-O Ranch, many old ranching features remain visible on trails.
- The West Peak Overlook offers stunning views of Bandera County's rugged hills.
- Stargazing here is exceptional due to minimal light pollution and open ridgelines.

Park Website

Park Maps

Visit the Texas Parks & Wildlife Department at tpwd.texas.gov

Honey Creek State Natural Area

3350 Park Rd 31, Spring Branch, TX 78070 - Hours: Guided Tour ONLY, Reservations REQUIRED

2X3 photo

History

Honey Creek State Natural Area was **established in 1985** to protect one of the clearest, most biologically diverse spring-fed streams in Central Texas. Flowing through limestone terrain and oak-juniper woodlands, Honey Creek is a vital part of the Guadalupe River watershed and feeds directly into the Edwards Aquifer recharge zone.

The area is co-managed by TPWD and conservation groups. To limit impact, the natural area is not open for hiking or unsupervised use. Instead, guided interpretive tours highlight the creek's ecology, geology, and cultural history, including native peoples and early German settlers.

Top Trails & Sites Visited

☐ Other: _______________________
☐ Other: _______________________
☐ Other: _______________________
☐ Other: _______________________

Guided Tour ONLY. No maps available to view online.

Date of Visit: ____

Where did you stay? ____

Who were you with? ____

What did you do? ____

Favorite Memories? ____

____

Interesting Facts

- Honey Creek is one of the purest streams in Texas, with consistent spring-fed flow and rare aquatic species.
- The natural area is home to the Golden-cheeked warbler, an endangered Hill Country songbird.
- Tours are led by naturalists through riparian woodlands, meadows, and canyon terrain.
- The creek flows directly into the Guadalupe River, just downstream of the park boundary.
- Honey Creek Cave nearby is one of the longest known caves in Texas (not publicly accessible).

State Park Stamp

Park Website

Park Maps

Visit the Texas Parks & Wildlife Department at tpwd.texas.gov

Hueco Tanks State Historic Site

6900 Hueco Tanks Rd #1, El Paso, TX 79938   -   Hours: Open daily from 8 AM to 6 PM

2X3 photo

History

Hueco Tanks is one of the most significant archaeological and cultural sites in Texas. Named for the natural rock basins ("huecos" in Spanish) that collect and store rainwater, the site has drawn human activity for over 10,000 years. It served as a critical water source for early hunter-gatherers, Puebloan peoples, Apache tribes, and later Spanish and Mexican settlers.

The park is especially known for its over 3,000 pictographs and petroglyphs, including rare masks from the Jornada Mogollon culture, which are protected by strict access rules. **It became a state historic site in 1969** and is now carefully managed for both cultural preservation and recreation.

Top Trails & Sites Visited

☐ Site 19 Trail (0.06 mi)
☐ North Mountain Trail (0.9 mi)
☐ Pond Trail (0.43 mi)
☐ Chain Trail (0.14 mi)
☐ Other: _______________________
☐ Other: _______________________

Date of Visit: ____

Where did you stay? ____

Who were you with? ____

What did you do? ____

Favorite Memories? ____

____

State Park Stamp

Interesting Facts

- Hueco Tanks is home to one of the largest concentrations of Native American rock art in Texas.
- Most of the park can only be accessed by guided tour or permit, preserving fragile areas.
- It's a world-class destination for bouldering, attracting climbers from around the globe.
- Visitors must watch a short orientation video before entry — part of its stewardship program.
- The huecos still hold rainwater year-round, supporting unique desert wildlife.

Park Website

Park Maps

Visit the Texas Parks & Wildlife Department at tpwd.texas.gov

Kickapoo Cavern State Park

20939 RR 674, Brackettville, TX 78832 - Hours: Open daily from 8 AM to 5 PM

2X3 photo

History

Kickapoo Cavern State Park encompasses over 6,300 acres of rugged limestone hills and desert habitat in the southwestern Hill Country. **Established in 1991, the** park was once a private ranch and includes 20 known caves, with Kickapoo Cavern and Stuart Bat Cave being the largest.

The park lies in the transition zone between the Edwards Plateau and the South Texas Plains, offering a blend of plant and animal species. It's a favorite for bat watching, birding, hiking, and geology enthusiasts looking for peace, beauty, and wild terrain.

Top Trails & Sites Visited

☐ Seargeant Memorial Trail (0.7 mi)
☐ Pine Canyon Loop (1.9 mi)
☐ Armadillo Lookout Trail (0.6 mi)
☐ Vireo Vista Trail (0.4 mi)
☐ Stuart Bat Cave
☐ Other: _______________________

Date of Visit: _______________________

Where did you stay? _______________________

Who were you with? _______________________

What did you do? _______________________

Favorite Memories? _______________________

____

Interesting Facts

- Kickapoo Cavern is over 1,400 feet long, featuring natural rooms, flowstone, and ceiling formations.
- Stuart Bat Cave hosts thousands of Mexican free-tailed bats from spring to fall — their evening flights are spectacular.
- The park is a top spot for birding, especially endangered species like the black-capped vireo.
- The area's limestone landscape includes sinkholes, creeks, and hidden springs.

State Park Stamp

Park Website

Park Maps

Visit the Texas Parks & Wildlife Department at tpwd.texas.gov

Lake Colorado City State Park

4582 FM 2836, Colorado City, TX 79512 - Hours: Open daily from 6 AM to 10 PM

2X3 photo

History

Lake Colorado City State Park was **established in 1972**, built around a reservoir originally created in the 1940s to serve a nearby power plant. Though the lake was man-made, the park provides a slice of brush country and semi-arid prairie, supporting a surprising variety of wildlife.

The lake was once used to cool the adjacent power plant (now decommissioned), and it retains warmer waters that attract both fish and waterfowl year-round. Today, the park is best known for its quiet campgrounds, boating access, and beautiful West Texas sunsets.

Top Trails & Sites Visited

☐ Cactus Cut Trail (1 mi)
☐ Roadrunner Loop Trail (2.1 mi)
☐ Rock Ridge
☐ Lakeview Dock
☐ Other: _______________________
☐ Other: _______________________

Date of Visit: _______________________________________

Where did you stay? _________________________________

Who were you with? _________________________________

What did you do? ____________________________________

Favorite Memories? __________________________________

State Park Stamp

Interesting Facts

- The park is home to javelinas, raccoons, roadrunners, and even occasional bobcats.
- It's a top destination for catching largemouth bass and catfish in the lake.
- There's a fishing pond for kids under 16 — no license required.
- In winter, the park becomes a haven for migrating ducks, geese, and shorebirds.
- You'll find some of the clearest stargazing skies anywhere in the region.

Park Website

Park Maps

Visit the Texas Parks & Wildlife Department at tpwd.texas.gov

Monahans Sandhills State Park

2500 Interstate 20 East, Monahans, TX 79756   -   Hours: Open daily from 8 AM to 10 PM

2X3 photo

History

Monahans Sandhills State Park was **established in 1957** to protect a portion of the Texas-New Mexico dune field, a massive system of shifting sand dunes stretching over 200 miles. The land here was once inhabited by Native tribes such as the Comanche and Apache, and later saw the arrival of railroads, ranchers, and oil developers.

Unlike most state parks, Monahans Sandhills is a semi-arid desert ecosystem with very little water — but tons of family-friendly fun. The dunes constantly move and change shape due to the wind, offering a dynamic, surreal landscape perfect for sandboarding, hiking, and photography.

Top Trails & Sites Visited
No formal trails — free-roaming encouraged

- ☐ Sand Dunes Exploration Area
- ☐ Shinoak Picnic Area
- ☐ Sunset & Stargazing Spots
- ☐ Other: _______________________
- ☐ Other: _______________________

Date of Visit: ____

Where did you stay? ____

Who were you with? ____

What did you do? ____

Favorite Memories? ____

____

____

Interesting Facts

- The tallest dunes can reach over 70 feet high and shift position over time.
- You can rent plastic sand discs at headquarters and sled down the dunes.
- The park protects a unique shinoak shrub forest, with deep root systems under the sand.
- You don't have to stay on trails — visitors are free to explore the dunes off-path.
- Despite being in oil country, the park offers peaceful silence and wide-open sky views.

State Park Stamp

Park Website

Park Maps

Visit the Texas Parks & Wildlife Department at tpwd.texas.gov

Old Tunnel State Park

10619 Old San Antonio Rd, Fredericksburg, TX 78624 - Hours: Open daily from Sunrise to 5PM

[2X3 photo]

History

Old Tunnel State Park preserves a stretch of the historic Fredericksburg and Northern Railway, which operated from 1913 to 1942. After the train line was abandoned, the abandoned railroad tunnel became home to millions of Mexican free tailed bats and several other bat species.

The area was designated a state park in 1991 to protect both the bats and the historic structure. Despite being the smallest state park in Texas (less than 20 acres), Old Tunnel offers one of the most memorable natural spectacles in the state — the nightly bat emergence during warm months.

Top Trails & Sites Visited

☐ Other: _______________________
☐ Other: _______________________
☐ Other: _______________________
☐ Other: _______________________
☐ Other: _______________________

Date of Visit: _______________________________________

Where did you stay? _______________________________________

Who were you with? _______________________________________

What did you do? _______________________________________

Favorite Memories? _______________________________________

____

____

State Park Stamp

Interesting Facts

- The park is home to over 3 million bats during peak season.
- The bats exit the tunnel in a swirling column at sunset, visible from late spring to early fall.
- The park contains part of the original railroad bed, now used as a short interpretive trail.
- It's a designated dark sky site, and bat programs often include stargazing.
- Daytime visitors can birdwatch, picnic, and explore native Hill Country plants.

Park Website

Park Maps

Visit the Texas Parks & Wildlife Department at tpwd.texas.gov

San Angelo State Park

362 South FM 2288, San Angelo, TX 76901   -   Hours: Open daily from 8 AM to 10 PM

2X3 photo

History

San Angelo State Park **opened in 1995**, surrounding the upper shores of O.C. Fisher Reservoir, a flood control lake built by the U.S. Army Corps of Engineers in the 1950s. The land was once home to Native American tribes like the Jumano and Lipan Apache, and later served as open ranching territory.

The park preserves a landscape of rolling mesquite-covered hills, shortgrass prairie, and rocky ridges typical of the Concho Valley and West Texas plains. It is also home to official herds of Texas longhorns and American bison, representing the state's natural and cultural heritage.

Top Trails & Sites Visited

- ☐ Pott's Creek Trail (1.6 mi) –
- ☐ Red Dam Loop (0.8 mi)
- ☐ Shady Trail (0.5 mi)
- ☐ Dinosaur Trail System (2.2 mi)
- ☐ Permian Tracks
- ☐ Other: _______________________

Date of Visit: ____

Where did you stay? ____

Who were you with? ____

What did you do? ____

Favorite Memories? ____

____

____

Interesting Facts

- The park maintains official Texas State Longhorn and Bison herds, which visitors can see up close.
- It features over 50 miles of trails for hiking, biking, and equestrian use.
- Home to O.C. Fisher Lake, which has dramatically fluctuated between dry bed and full pool.
- Excellent for stargazing and sunrise photography thanks to wide-open skies.
- You can reserve the Red Arroyo Pavilion, a scenic shaded overlook area, for events.

State Park Stamp

Park Website

Park Maps

Visit the Texas Parks & Wildlife Department at tpwd.texas.gov

Seminole Canyon State Park

US Hwy 90 W, Comstock, TX 78837 – Hours: Open daily from 8 AM to 4:30 PM

2X3 photo

History

Seminole Canyon State Park preserves a dramatic landscape where ancient peoples left their mark. Human habitation in this area dates back over 10,000 years, and its most famous attraction is the Fate Bell Shelter, which contains rock art estimated to be over 8,000 years old.

The park was **established in 1980** to protect this cultural heritage and includes wide views of the Rio Grande canyonlands. The area also preserves military and frontier history — including the nearby route of the Black Seminole Scouts, for whom the canyon is named.

Top Trails & Sites Visited

- ☐ Birding Trail (0.1 mi)
- ☐ Canyon Rim Trail (4.9 mi)
- ☐ Middle Fork Trail (0.8 mi)
- ☐ Rio Grande Trail (2.3 mi)
- ☐ Rio Grande View
- ☐ Other: ________________________

Date of Visit: ____

Where did you stay? ____

Who were you with? ____

What did you do? ____

Favorite Memories? ____

____

State Park Stamp

Interesting Facts

- The park is home to some of the oldest Native American pictographs in North America.
- The Fate Bell Shelter is only accessible by guided tour, due to its fragility and significance.
- The park's name honors the Black Seminole Scouts, U.S. Army troops who patrolled the area in the 1870s.
- The Rio Grande and Pecos River junction is just downstream of the park boundary.
- You can see into Mexico from high points along the canyon rim.

Park Website

Park Maps

Visit the Texas Parks & Wildlife Department at tpwd.texas.gov

Wyler Aerial Tramway

1700 McKinley Ave, El Paso, TX 79930 - Access to park is ONLY allowed during guided programs
Check the website calendar for upcoming events

2X3 photo

History

The Wyler Aerial Tramway opened to the public in **1960** as a private attraction before being donated to the state by Karl O. Wyler in 1997. It became a Texas State Park in 2001. The tram carried passengers up to Ranger Peak, offering sweeping views of El Paso, Mexico, and New Mexico.

At its peak, the tramway climbed nearly 1,000 feet in elevation in just 4 minutes. Although closed since 2018 due to mechanical concerns, the site remains under state management.

Top Trails & Sites Visited

- ☐ Directissimo Trail (0.5 mi)
- ☐ Ranger Peak Loop Trail (1.4 mi)
- ☐ Thousand Steps Trail (1.6 mi)
- ☐ B-36D Bomber His. Crash Site
- ☐ Ranger Peak Observation
- ☐ Other: _______________________

Date of Visit: ____

Where did you stay? _______________________________________

Who were you with? _______________________________________

What did you do? ____

Favorite Memories? _______________________________________

____

____

Interesting Facts

- At the summit, visitors could see 3 states and 2 countries from one viewpoint.
- The tramway cabins held up to 8 people and ran on 2,600 feet of cable.
- Ranger Peak stands at 5,632 feet above sea level, one of the highest accessible points in El Paso.
- The attraction was named for Karl Wyler, a broadcasting pioneer and local philanthropist.
- While the tram is closed, hiking access to Ranger Peak is still possible via Franklin Mountains trails.

State Park Stamp

Park Website

Park Maps

Visit the Texas Parks & Wildlife Department at tpwd.texas.gov

Caprock Canyons State Park

850 Caprock Canyon Park Road, Quitaque, TX 79255 - Hours: Open daily from 8 AM to 10 PM

2X3 photo

History

Caprock Canyons State Park was **established in 1982** and preserves a stunning landscape of red rock cliffs, canyons, mesas, and prairie grasslands. The land lies at the edge of the Llano Estacado, where the flat high plains suddenly drop off into rugged canyon country.

The park is also home to the Texas State Bison Herd, a genetically pure group of southern plains bison descended from animals cared for by pioneer Charles Goodnight. The herd now roams freely within a large portion of the park — making Caprock one of the most unique wildlife destinations in Texas.

Top Trails & Sites Visited

☐ Mesa Trail (3.1 mi)
☐ Canyon Rim Trail (3.0 mi)
☐ Eagle Point Trail (2.0 mi)
☐ North Prong Spur (1.3 mi)
☐ Haynes Ridge Overlook (2.5 mi)
☐ Other: _______________________

Date of Visit: _______________________

Where did you stay? _______________________

Who were you with? _______________________

What did you do? _______________________

Favorite Memories? _______________________

State Park Stamp

Interesting Facts

- Caprock Canyons is home to Texas's official bison herd, which roams throughout the park.
- The park includes a section of the Caprock Canyons Trailway, a 64-mile multi-use trail on a former railroad.
- It features geological formations formed over millions of years, including hoodoos and cathedral spires.
- The area is a top spot for bat watching — thousands emerge nightly from nearby Clarity Tunnel.
- You can hike to Fern Cave, where a small desert spring nourishes a moss-covered wall inside a canyon.

Park Website   Park Maps

Visit the Texas Parks & Wildlife Department at tpwd.texas.gov

Copper Breaks State Park

777 State Hwy Park Rd 62, Quanah, TX 79252 – Hours: Open daily from 8 AM to 10 PM

[2X3 photo]

History

Copper Breaks State Park **opened in 1974** and is named for its distinctive copper-colored soils and rocky outcrops. The land once belonged to the Comanche and Kiowa peoples before becoming ranchland and later a protected park.

Set within the Rolling Plains and featuring both canyon breaks and mesquite grasslands, the park offers a quiet escape for campers, hikers, and night sky enthusiasts. It is one of Texas's official International Dark Sky Parks, making it ideal for meteor showers and stargazing.

Top Trails & Sites Visited

- ☐ Juniper Ridge Nature Trail (0.7 mi)
- ☐ Bull Canyon Short Loop (1.0 mi)
- ☐ Juniper Ridge Overlook
- ☐ Permian Sea Tide Ripples
- ☐ Other: _______________________
- ☐ Other: _______________________

Date of Visit: ____

Where did you stay? ____

Who were you with? ____

What did you do? ____

Favorite Memories? ____

____

Interesting Facts

- The park is home to a portion of the official State Longhorn Herd of Texas.
- Its International Dark Sky designation makes it a favorite for stargazing and astrophotography.
- Two lakes — Big Pond and Lake Copper Breaks — offer fishing and paddling.
- The park's rugged geology includes red-orange cliffs, mesas, and eroded gullies.
- It's one of the least crowded state parks — great for solitude and photography.

State Park Stamp

Park Website

Park Maps

Visit the Texas Parks & Wildlife Department at tpwd.texas.gov

Lake Arrowhead State Park

229 Park Road 63, Wichita Falls, TX 76310 - Hours: Open daily from 6 AM to 10 PM

2X3 photo

History

Lake Arrowhead State Park **opened in 1970** and offers visitors easy access to Lake Arrowhead, a reservoir built in the 1960s for water supply to the city of Wichita Falls. The park was developed to give locals a place to enjoy nature, boating, and shoreline fishing — with open skies and wide prairie views.

The area was once part of the Texas Blackland Prairie and still supports many native grasses, wildflowers, and songbirds. Today, it's known for its quiet campgrounds, relaxed boating, and prime fishing year-round.

Top Trails & Sites Visited

- ☐ Mesquite Ridge Trail (0.6 mi)
- ☐ Onion Creek Trail (4.4 mi)
- ☐ Dragonfly Trail (0.5 mi)
- ☐ "The Horn" Tunnel
- ☐ Oil Well Pumpjack
- ☐ Other: ______________________

Date of Visit: _______________________________________

Where did you stay? _______________________________________

Who were you with? _______________________________________

What did you do? _______________________________________

Favorite Memories? _______________________________________

____

____

State Park Stamp

Interesting Facts

- A large prairie dog town sits near the entrance — great for wildlife viewing and photos.
- The park has an ADA-accessible fishing pier and shoreline designed for bank fishing.
- It's a top location for catching catfish, crappie, and hybrid striped bass.
- The prairie blooms with Texas bluebonnets and wildflowers in spring.
- Butterflies, hawks, and dragonflies fill the skies in warmer months.

Park Website   Park Maps

Visit the Texas Parks & Wildlife Department at tpwd.texas.gov

Palo Duro Canyon State Park

11450 Park Road 5, Canyon, TX 79015 - Hours: Open daily from 7:30 AM to 9 PM

2X3 photo

History

Palo Duro Canyon is the second largest state park system. **The park opened in 1934**, with much of its early development done by the Civilian Conservation Corps (CCC).

Before colonization, the canyon was home to Comanche, Kiowa, and Apache peoples. In 1874, Red River War caused families to move up the canyon. The canyon's vivid, colorful layers, hoodoos, and open trails now make it a favorite for geology lovers, hikers, and photographers.

Top Trails & Sites Visited

- ☐ Pioneer Nature Trail (0.4 mi)
- ☐ Rojo Grande Trail (1.2 mi)
- ☐ Sunflower Trail (1.2 mi)
- ☐ Lighthouse Trail (5.6 mi)
- ☐ Other: _______________________
- ☐ Other: _______________________

Date of Visit: ____

Where did you stay? ____

Who were you with? ____

What did you do? ____

Favorite Memories? ____

____

____

Interesting Facts

- The canyon stretches 120 miles long, up to 20 miles wide, and drops 800 feet deep.
- The park is home to the famous Lighthouse Rock, a natural formation reached by trail.
- CCC workers built many original roads and structures, still in use today.
- The outdoor amphitheater hosts "TEXAS," a long-running musical drama about Texas history.
- Wildlife includes Aoudad sheep, wild turkeys, roadrunners, bobcats, and tarantulas.

State Park Stamp

Park Website   Park Maps

Visit the Texas Parks & Wildlife Department at tpwd.texas.gov

Brazos Bend State Park

21901 FM 762, Needville, TX 77461 – Hours: Open daily from 8 AM to 10 PM

2X3 photo

History

Located on land once used by indigenous Karankawa tribes and later settled by ranchers, Brazos Bend's rich wetlands and prairies were preserved by Texas Parks & Wildlife Department after acquisition in the late 1970s. **The park officially opened in 1984.**

Evidence of early human activity dating back thousands of years has been found here. Today, the park is known for its thriving ecosystems and commitment to conservation education, supported by an active volunteer base and partnership with the Houston Museum of Natural Science's George Observatory.

Top Trails & Sites Visited

- ☐ Elm Lake Trail (1.7 mi)
- ☐ Pilant Slough Trail (1.2 mi)
- ☐ Prairie Trail (1.3 mi)
- ☐ Creekfield Lake Trail (0.5 mi)
- ☐ George Observatory
- ☐ Other:___________________

Date of Visit: ____

Where did you stay? ____

Who were you with? ____

What did you do? ____

Favorite Memories? ____

____

____

State Park Stamp

Interesting Facts

- Just 45 miles from Houston, yet spans over 4,800 acres of forests, prairies, and lakes.
- Famous for its large population of American alligators, especially around Elm Lake.
- Hosts the George Observatory, offering night sky viewing events through powerful telescopes.
- Offers over 37 miles of trails for hiking, biking, and horseback riding.
- One of the top birding sites in Texas, drawing wildlife photographers and birdwatchers year-round.

Park Website   Park Maps

Visit the Texas Parks & Wildlife Department at tpwd.texas.gov

Galveston Island State Park

14901 FM 3005, Galveston, TX 77554 - Hours: Open daily from 7 AM to 10 PM

2X3 photo

History

Galveston Island State Park was **officially opened in 1975**. Long before Spanish colonization, the Karankawa people inhabited the island, relying on fishing, shellfish, and sea birds for survival. During the 1800s, Galveston Island became a thriving port and resort destination — but also endured severe hurricanes, including the devastating storm of 1900.

The land that now forms the state park was once a barrier of sand dunes, tidal flats, and freshwater wetlands — threatened in the 20th century by rapid coastal development. Conservationists stepped in to protect the area's unique coastal habitat. After extensive damage from Hurricane Ike in 2008, the park underwent a major rebuilding process, with a full beach side restoration completed in 2012.

Top Trails & Sites Visited

☐ Clapper Rail Loop (1.4 mi)
☐ Caracara Trail (0.9 mi)
☐ Eskimo Curlew Loop (0.5 mi)
☐ Heritage Trail (0.3 mi)
☐ Alligator Loop (1.0 mi)
☐ Other:_______________________

Date of Visit: ____

Where did you stay? ____

Who were you with? ____

What did you do? ____

Favorite Memories? ____

____

Interesting Facts

- The park stretches from Gulf beach to bay, offering two very different ecosystems.
- You can kayak through coastal marshes and fish from both surf and bay.
- The park has over 2,000 acres of restored barrier island habitat.
- The Nature Center hosts free family programs and wildlife viewing.
- A hotspot for migratory birds, especially during spring and fall.

State Park Stamp

Park Website

Park Maps

Goose Island State Park

202 S. Palmetto St., Rockport, TX 78382 - Hours: Open daily from 8 AM to 10 PM

2X3 photo

History

Goose Island State Park **opened in 1931**, making it one of the earliest state parks in Texas. Built in part by the Civilian Conservation Corps, the park protects a unique mix of coastal prairie, oak motts, tidal flats, and marshlands along St. Charles and Aransas Bays.

Perhaps the park's most iconic feature is the "Big Tree," a massive coastal live oak estimated to be over 1,000 years old. Goose Island also became a haven for conservation during the mid-20th century, particularly for protecting whooping cranes, which winter in the nearby Aransas National Wildlife Refuge.

Top Trails & Sites Visited

- ☐ Turks Cap Trail (0.66 mi)
- ☐ St. Charles Bay
- ☐ Aransas Bay
- ☐ Other: _______________________
- ☐ Other: _______________________
- ☐ Other: _______________________

Date of Visit: _______________________

Where did you stay? _______________________

Who were you with? _______________________

What did you do? _______________________

Favorite Memories? _______________________

____

____

State Park Stamp

Interesting Facts

- The park is home to the "Big Tree", one of the largest and oldest live oak trees in the U.S.
- It's a birding paradise — especially in winter when rare whooping cranes migrate nearby.
- The 1,620-foot lighted fishing pier is open 24/7 and a favorite for night anglers.
- You can camp right on the bay, with sea breezes and water views.
- The park is near Rockport, a vibrant coastal town with seafood, art, and beach access.

Park Website

Park Maps

Visit the Texas Parks & Wildlife Department at tpwd.texas.gov

Powderhorn State Park

FM 1289 & Powderhorn Lake, Port O'Connor, TX 77982 – Hours: Open daily from ___AM to ___PM

2X3 photo

History

Powderhorn State Park is being developed on over 17,000 acres of pristine Gulf Coast prairie, purchased in 2014 through one of the largest conservation land acquisitions in Texas history.

Previously known as the Powderhorn Ranch, the land was protected through a coalition of public and private partners, including TPWD, The Nature Conservancy, and Texas Parks and Wildlife Foundation. The site is already open for research and wildlife management and is expected to become a flagship destination for birding, paddling, fishing, and coastal habitat conservation. Opened ________________.

Top Trails & Sites Visited

- ☐
- ☐
- ☐
- ☐ Other: _______________________
- ☐ Other: _______________________
- ☐ Other: _______________________

Date of Visit: ____

Where did you stay? ____

Who were you with? ____

What did you do? ____

Favorite Memories? ____

Interesting Facts

- The park includes over 11 miles of shoreline along Matagorda Bay and Powderhorn Lake.
- It protects one of the largest intact coastal prairies remaining in Texas.
- More than 300 bird species have been documented here, including roseate spoonbills and whooping cranes.
- The land acquisition was valued at over $50 million.
- A portion of the site is already managed as a Wildlife Management Area (WMA) for research and habitat protection.

State Park Stamp

Park Website

Park Maps

Visit the Texas Parks & Wildlife Department at tpwd.texas.gov

Sea Rim State Park

19335 TX-87, Sabine Pass, TX 77655 - Hours: Open daily from 7 AM to 10 PM

2X3 photo

History

Sea Rim State Park protects over 4,000 acres of Gulf Coast marshlands and beachfront. Once used by Native American tribes and later settlers for fishing and shellfish gathering, the area remained wild until the mid-20th century. **It was officially opened as a state park in 1977** to protect fragile wetland and barrier island ecosystems that had rapidly declined due to coastal development.

Hurricanes Rita (2005) and Ike (2008) devastated the park, closing it for several years. Since reopening, Sea Rim has become a model for coastal restoration — with boardwalks, elevated trails, and birding blinds allowing visitors to experience this unique marsh-meets-Gulf landscape.

Top Trails & Sites Visited

- ☐ Gambusia Nature Trail (0.9 mi)
- ☐ Dune Boardwalk (0.1 mi)
- ☐ Easy Paddling Trail (1.8 mi)
- ☐ Moderate Paddling Trail (4.7 mi)
- ☐ Advanced Paddling Trail (11.7 mi)
- ☐ Other:________________________

Date of Visit: ___________________________________

Where did you stay? _______________________________

Who were you with? _______________________________

What did you do? _________________________________

Favorite Memories? _______________________________

____

State Park Stamp

Interesting Facts

- Sea Rim has over 5 miles of natural Gulf shoreline, where you can look for shells and spot stingrays.
- The park offers elevated boardwalk blinds for prime birdwatching, especially during migration seasons.
- The Gambusia boardwalk trail crosses several brackish ponds known to attract alligators, frogs, and rabbits.
- Sea Rim is one of the few Texas state parks where you can paddle through a freshwater marsh and walk on the beach in the same visit.

Park Website

Park Maps

Visit the Texas Parks & Wildlife Department at tpwd.texas.gov

Stephen F. Austin State Park

Park Road 38, San Felipe, TX 77473 - Hours: Open daily from 8 AM to 10 PM

2X3 photo

History

Stephen F. Austin State Park sits on land steeped in early Texas history. The park is located near the site of San Felipe de Austin. In the 1820s and 1830s, this area was a bustling hub for settlers moving into Mexican Texas. The town played a pivotal role in the Texas Revolution but was ultimately burned in 1836 by retreating Texan forces to keep it out of Mexican hands.

In 1940, the land was donated to the state, and the park was established to honor Austin's legacy and preserve the site of Texas' earliest settlements. Though the original town was never fully rebuilt, interpretive signs, historical markers, and nearby exhibits help tell the story of the people who shaped the state's early destiny.

Top Trails & Sites Visited

- ☐ Ironwood Trail (1 mi)
- ☐ Barred Owl Trail (0.7 mi)
- ☐ Sycamore Trail (0.5 mi)
- ☐ Pileated Trail (.7 mi)
- ☐ Historic Townsite ruins
- ☐ Other:_______________________

Date of Visit: ____

Where did you stay? ____

Who were you with? ____

What did you do? ____

Favorite Memories? ____

____

Interesting Facts

- Includes a 12-acre historic site now managed by the Texas Historical Commission.
- A popular stop on New Year's First Day Hikes, offering scenic winter trails.
- A small on-site 9-hole golf course is available—unusual for a Texas state park

State Park Stamp

Park Website

Park Maps

Visit the Texas Parks & Wildlife Department at tpwd.texas.gov

Alphabetical List of Texas State Parks

Alphabetical List of Texas State Parks

Texas State Parks Pass

Explore More. Save More.

If you plan to visit several state parks in Texas, the Texas State Parks Pass is a great investment for individuals, families, and frequent explorers.

This annual pass is available for $70 and provides unlimited free entry to more than 80+ Texas State Parks for one year. It covers not only the cardholder, but everyone in the same vehicle.

Benefits of the Texas State Parks Pass:
- Free daily entrance to all Texas state parks for the passholder and guests in the same vehicle
- Discounts on camping, park store purchases, equipment rentals, and more!

Passes can be purchased online, at any Texas state park, or by calling the Texas Parks and Wildlife Department.

For the most current details or to purchase a pass with TPWD, scan the QR code below to visit: